A Z-80 WORKSHOP MANUAL

G000240816

by
E. A. PARR
B.Sc., C.Eng., M.I.E.E.

BERNARD BABANI (publishing) LTD
THE GRAMPIANS
SHEPHERDS BUSH ROAD
LONDON W6 7NF
ENGLAND

PLEASE NOTE

© 1983 BERNARD BABANI (publishing) LTD

First Published – July 1983
Reprinted – July 1986
Reprinted – October 1989

British Library Cataloguing in Publication Data
Parr, E. A.
   A Z-80 workshop manual. – (BP112)
   1. INTEL Z-80 (Computer)
   I. Title
   001.64'04   QA76.8.I/

ISBN 0 85934 087 2

Printed and bound in Great Britain by Cox & Wyman Ltd, Reading

INTRODUCTION

Although there are many contenders for the title of "most successful micro", the Z-80 has been universally acclaimed as the most powerful and versatile 8 bit microprocessor. It is found in many popular microcomputers, including the Nascom, TRS-80, ZX-80/81, Spectrum, Video Genie, Sharp MZ-80K and Cromenco machines.

This book has been written for owners of Z-80 based machines who have become reasonably proficient in BASIC, and wish to progress to machine code and assembler language programming. This can be a rather daunting task, as most Z-80 literature has been designed for computer professionals and is not readily understandable.

The book has also been designed to be a general introduction to machine code programming. All the popular microprocessors such as the 6502, 6800 etc. use similar techniques to the Z-80. Once the Z-80 has been mastered, the reader will have little problem with its simpler cousins. It is therefore hoped that the book will also prove useful to anyone who is simply interested in computing.

ACKNOWLEDGEMENTS

This book is about the Zilog Z-80 microprocessor, and contains all the detail necessary for the average enthusiast to gain insight into any Z-80 based microcomputer. It follows that much of the information given has been obtained from Zilog, and their assistance is greatly appreciated.

It should be noted that Zilog, Z-80 and the various micro-computers and assembler/monitor names referred to in the text are registered trade marks.

My wife Alison, has, as usual, been long suffering; not only putting up with the computers in the house, but also doing my typing despite a house move over the length of the United Kingdom.

Andrew Parr.
Minster,
Isle of Sheppey.

CONTENTS

Chapter One

THE MICROCOMPUTER

1.1 INTRODUCTION

A computer based on the Z-80 operates in the same manner as
any other machine be it micro, mini or mainframe. Before we
can discuss the Z-80 and its use in any detail, it is first necessary to describe the operation of a typical microcomputer.
This will serve to define the terms used in the rest of the book,
and place the Z-80 in its role as the central processor of a
powerful, but conventional computer.

1.2 COMPUTER ARCHITECTURE

All computers can be represented by the block diagram of
Fig.1.1, and can be considered as manipulators of data. The
actual form of the data will depend on the application. In
commercial computing the data will be VAT returns, sales
figures, bank accounts and similar information. In industrial
control, the data will be plant sensors and actuators. In a
computer game the data will be the players hand controls and
the video display. The data can be split into input data, which
is to be processed, and the output data, which is the result
of the processing. To produce the output data, the computer
follows a set of procedures, called instructions, which define
the operations that are to be performed on the input data.

The computer can be represented in more detail by Fig.1.2,
and can be considered to consist of three basic units; a store,
an input/output unit and a central processor unit, all inter-
connected by a common highway. The input and output unit
obviously receives and transmits data from and to the outside
world. The store is used to hold instructions and data. The
central processor unit controls the operation of the machine,
and performs the logic and arithmetic operations required
by the instructions.

1

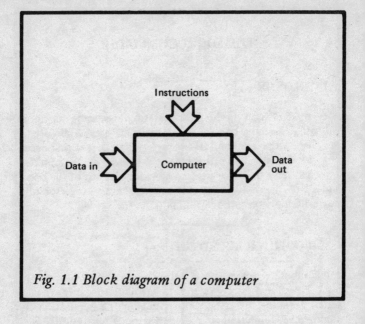

Fig. 1.1 Block diagram of a computer

1.3 THE STORE

The store is used to hold the instructions and temporary data in the form of numbers. It can best be considered as an array of pigeon holes, each of which can hold one number called (rather confusingly) a Word. Each pigeon hole is known as a store location, and has a unique address (similar to a house address) by which it can be identified. We can thus say, for example, "store location 3220 contains 127". This means that the pigeon hole whose address is 3220 has the number 127 stored in it.

A typical microcomputer will have over 16000 store locations (although small machines may have less than 1000). All common microprocessors deal basically with 8 bit numbers, often called Bytes. The numbers stored will therefore be in the range 0 to 255. As will be seen later, this is not the restriction that it might at first appear.

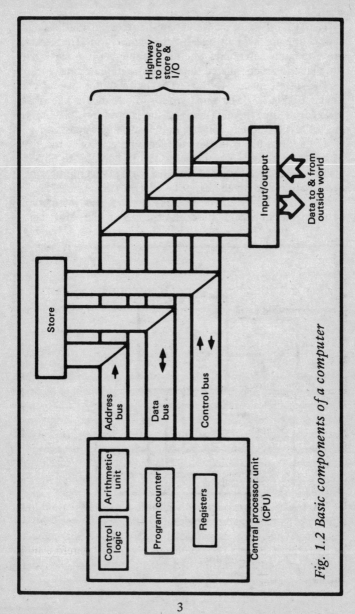

Fig. 1.2 Basic components of a computer

The store does not differentiate between instructions and data; both are held in exactly the same form. The central processor unit determines whether the number in a particular store location is considered to be an instruction or data.

The store connects to the rest of the computer in a manner similar to Fig.1.3. The three groups of signals are known as the address bus, the data bus and the control bus. (The term bus is short for busbar, sometimes the term highway is used.)

The address bus is used by the central processor to identify which store address is to be accessed. Usually, up to 65,536 (called 64K) locations can be used with a microprocessor, necessitating a 16 bit address bus.

The data bus is used to transfer data and instruction between the store and the central processor unit. Movement

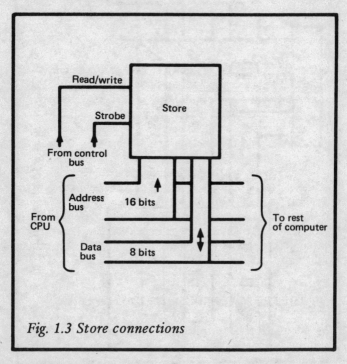

Fig. 1.3 Store connections

can take place from store to CPU, or CPU to store, so the data bus is bidirectional. All common microprocessors use an 8 bit data bus.

The control bus contains the timing signals to sequence the movement of data or instructions. In the majority of systems there are basically two signals. A read/write line is used to indicate if a number is to be loaded into or read from, the addressed location, and a strobe signal indicates when the number on the data bus is valid (i.e. the transients due to different propagation delays, reflections etc. have died away). Different microprocessors use slightly different signals.

Fig.1.4a summarises the signals used to write a store location, and Fig.1.4b the signals used to read from a store location.

When a number is written to a store location, the previous contents are obviously overwritten. When a number is read from a store location, the store location contents are unaltered; the number put onto the data bus is merely a *COPY* of the store contents.

The store in Fig.1.3 is known as a RAM or Random Access Memory. This is a term that causes some confusion, but simply means that each store location can be accessed in exactly the same time. Bulk storage devices, such as tapes and discs, have a variable access time which depends on where the information is stored and where the tape or disc currently is when the information is needed.

Another form of storage commonly encountered is a ROM, for Read Only Memory. This is a conventional store whose contents are fixed and cannot be altered by the computer. Usually a ROM is used to hold a fixed program (such as the BASIC interpreter or an Assembler as described later). To the central processor, a ROM behaves in exactly the same manner as the rest of the store.

1.4   THE CENTRAL PROCESSOR UNIT (or CPU)

The computer follows instructions held in the store (in the form of numbers). Normally, instructions are held in

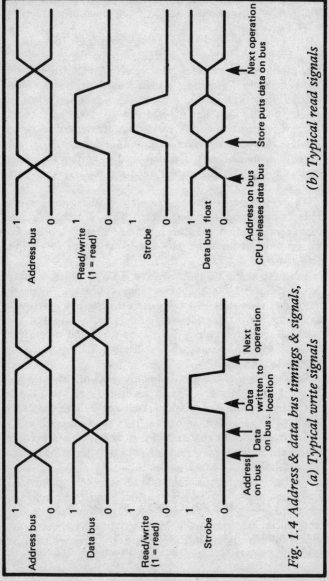

Fig. 1.4 Address & data bus timings & signals,

(a) Typical write signals

Address bus 1 / 0
Data bus 1 / 0
Read/write 1 / 0 (1 = read)
Strobe 1 / 0

Address on bus | Data on bus | Data written to bus location | Next operation

(b) Typical read signals

Address bus 1 / 0
Read/write 1 / 0 (1 = read)
Strobe 1 / 0
Data bus float 1 / 0

Address on bus CPU releases data bus | Store puts data on bus | Next operation puts data on bus

sequential store locations. To obey an instruction we must go through the following steps:

i. Address the store to get the next instruction.
ii. Decode the instruction to decide what needs to be done
iii. Obey the instruction. This will usually involve the store again to read, or write, data and will often require simple arithmetic operations
iv. Decide where the next instruction is held in the store, and go back to step i.

Most instructions therefore require two operations on the store; the first to read the instruction, the second to read the data to be used or write a result back to the store. Sometimes the operations above are referred to as three steps:-

Fetch cycle (instruction is fetched, steps i and ii)
Execute cycle (instruction is obeyed, step iii)
Reset cycle (the internal logic is reset for the next instruction, step iv)

The FER sequence has been called the heartbeat of a computer.

The component parts of a central processor unit are shown on Fig.1.5. For simplification, internal connections are omitted.

The program counter (PC, also known as an instruction counter, IC) holds the address of the current instruction. Because most microcomputers can address up to 64K, the PC will usually be a 16 bit register. With the exception of JUMP instructions (the machine code equivalent of a BASIC GOTO instruction), the program will be held in sequential store locations. This means that the PC can literally be a counter which is pulsed by the control logic at step iv above.

In addition to the storage provided by the RAM, fast storage (for temporary scribbling pad purposes) is provided by registers in the CPU. These can hold one number to the same word length as the store (8 bits for all common micros). Some microprocessors (such as the 6502) have only one register, whereas some (such as the Z-80) have as many as sixteen. Fig.1.5 shows four registers for illustrative purposes.

7

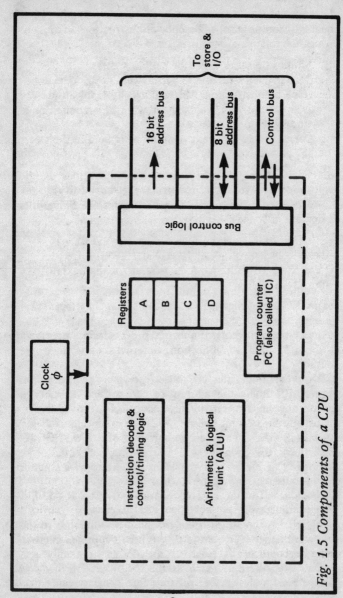

Fig. 1.5 Components of a CPU

The use of registers will be described later.

Associated with the registers is the Arithmetic and Logic Unit (or ALU). There are actually very few machine code instructions; as we shall see later, most are variations on:

Fetch a number from a store location (or input port) to a register

Write a number to a store location (or output port) from a register

Add (or subtract) a number from a store location to a register, result to a register.

The ALU performs the arithmetical operations (and some logical operations such as AND, OR) required by the instructions.

Finally, we have the block labelled control/timing logic. This contains the logic to decode the instructions and sequence the steps i to iv above. This involves selecting routes between the store, the ALU, the registers and the highways. The control/timing logic is usually the most complex part of a computer.

Associated with the control logic is a simple clock oscillator which provides the basic timing pulses. Usually this is a crystal oscillator in the range 1 to 4MHz.

A microprocessor is often thought of as a computer, but is, in fact, simply the CPU of a computer. A microprocessor contains the elements of Fig.1.5, but needs external RAM/ROM and Input/Output equipment to be useful.

1.5 INPUT AND OUTPUT

A computer connects to a variety of I/O equipment, printers, keyboards, VDUs, cassette recorders etc. These connect to the computer highway as shown on Fig.1.6. Each I/O device is identified by an address. I/O addresses are commonly known as 'Ports', so we could have, say, a printer connected to Port 3 and a keyboard to Port 5.

Data is transferred to and from an I/O port via the highway. The port address is placed on the address highway, the read/

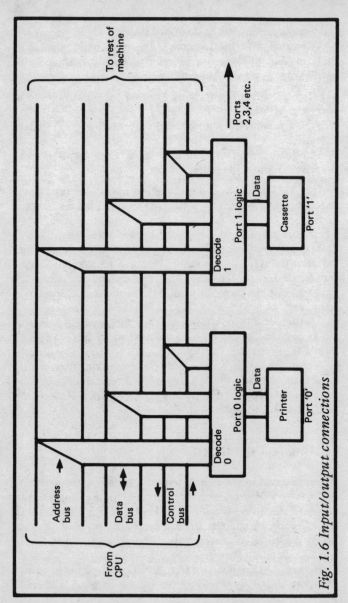

Fig. 1.6 Input/output connections

write control line used to identify the direction of the transfer, and the I/O control line used to signify that the address is a port address, not a store address. Data transfer then takes place via the data highway. Some microprocessors (such as the 6800) do not have an I/O control line and literally deal with I/O addresses in the same ways and with the same instructions, as store addresses. With these microprocessors a store and a port cannot have the same address.

Most microprocessors allow data to be transferred between I/O ports and registers or between I/O ports and store locations. We shall discuss later the techniques used to resolve the vast difference in speed between slow speed devices (such as printers) and the computer itself.

1.6 INSTRUCTIONS AND PROGRAMS

As anyone who has written a program in BASIC will know, a computer simply obeys a sequence of instructions called a program. In a high level language such as BASIC or PASCAL, these instructions are written in 'English'. A computer actually obeys instructions represented by numbers called a machine code program. When a high level program is obeyed, a special program built into the computer (called a compiler or an interpreter) converts the high level language program to an equivalent machine code program. This action is invisible to the high level language user.

A machine code instruction must specify:

i. What is to be done (e.g. Add, fetch data, store data, etc.)
ii. Where the data is to be found, and where the result is to be placed (e.g. "Fetch the data from store location 2000 to Register B", or "Add the data in store location 1575 to the data in Register A putting the result in Register A").

In following chapters we will see how these ideas are actually specified given the limitations of an 8 bit word.

There are actually a very limited set of instructions in a computer, and most are variations on:

1.6.1 Fetch

"Fetch data from a specified store location (or register) to a specified register".

1.6.2 Store

"Store data from a specified register to a specified store location". Sometimes Fetch and Store are collectively called "Moves" or "Loads".

1.6.3 Add

"Add data from a specified store location (or register) to the data in another specified store location (or register) the result to go to a specified store location (or register)".

Usually Adds take the simpler form, "Add data from a specified store location to the data in register A, the result to go to Register A".

1.6.4 Subtract

As 1.6.3 but subtraction is performed. Note that multiplication and division are not available on any common microprocessor.

1.6.5 Logical

As 1.6.3, but logical operations such as AND, OR, NEV are performed between the data.

1.6.6 Shifts

Data in a microprocessor is held as 8 bit binary numbers. A shift instruction moves the data in a register up, or down by one place. If we have the bit pattern 10110101, a simple shift up would produce 01101010, and simple shift down would produce 01011010. A shift up multiplies a number by two, a shift down divides by two. As will be seen later, there are many variations on the shift instruction.

1.6.7 Jumps

Normally, instructions are held in sequential store locations. A Jump instruction is the machine code equivalent of the BASIC GOTO, and specifies where the next instruction is to be found (e.g. Jump to location 3220).

1.6.8 Conditional Jump

A conditional jump tests the condition of a register, the results of which determine if a jump instruction is to be obeyed (e.g. Jump to 4057 if register A is zero). This is the machine code equivalent to the BASIC IF condition THEN GOTO (line number).

1.6.9 Subroutine Call and Return

Programmers in BASIC will be familiar with the concept of a subroutine with the GOSUB and RETURN instructions. A subroutine allows a piece of program that is used frequently to be written once and called when needed by the rest of the program. This is best shown by Fig.1.7. Machine code subroutine calls work in exactly the same way. A subroutine call acts like a jump to the start of the subroutine (e.g. Call 7087 would take us to the subroutine starting at location 7087). A Return instruction is placed at the end of the subroutine, to take us back to the location in the main program immediately after the subroutine call. Subroutines can call subroutines (called Nesting). A Binary to BCD subroutine, for example, would need to use multiplication and division subroutines. In most microprocessors, conditional subroutine calls, and conditional returns are provided as well as the simple call and return described above.

1.6.10 Input/Output Instructions

Input/output instructions must specify the I/O port address,

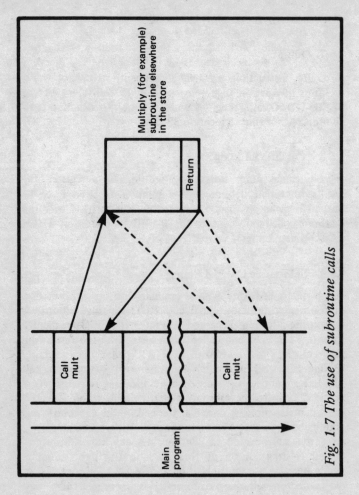

Fig. 1.7 The use of subroutine calls

the direction (in or out) and the source (or destination) of the data (i.e. which register or which store location).

1.6.11 Control Instructions

Most microprocessors have a small number of control instructions such as STOP, Disable Interrupts and similar operations. These do not involve data.

At first sight, the vast array of instructions available on a microprocessor can be rather awe inspiring (the Z-80 has 158 different instruction types). Much of the inevitable feeling of confusion can be assuaged by remembering that most instructions are simple variations of the ten types outlined above.

1.7   WHY MACHINE CODE?

Programming in BASIC is simple and straightforward, so it is not unreasonable to ask why one should bother with the trials, tribulations and complexity of machine code programming. There are really three reasons.

The first is that it is possible to perform operations in machine code that are impossible (or difficult) to achieve in BASIC. Control of external items like a model railway would be difficult in simple BASIC for example.

The second reason concerns speed. BASIC is notoriously slow, and is quite unsuited to, say dynamic video games. Machine code programs operate many times faster than BASIC programs.

The final and most compelling, reason is that machine code programming is an intellectual challenge akin to chess or bridge. The mental exercise of programming (in any form) is very addictive and this is particularly true of machine code programs.

1.8   MACHINE CODE AND ASSEMBLERS

The instructions a computer actually obeys are held in the form of binary numbers. To assist human beings to read these numbers, it is usual to express them in Hex, so 1010 0111 becomes A7 (see Appendix A).

A machine code program therefore looks something like:

F5 C5 D6 64 3E Z0 D3 00 etc.

which is still fairly incomprehensible.

It is easier to follow a machine code program if simple mnemonics are used to represent the instructions. The actual mnemonics used on the Z-80 will be described later, but in general they are simple to understand. A program written in mnemonics is said to be written in Assembler Language, and looks more understandable.

> LD A, 33
> INC HL
> JP NZ, LOOP

Each of these corresponds directly to a single machine code intruction, LD A,33 for example, means put the number 33 into register A.

The program written in Assembler Mnemonics is converted to machine code by a program called (surprise, surprise) an Assembler. The Assembler has editing facilities similar to those found in BASIC and makes machine code programming much less infuriating. In later chapters, examples of Assembler programs will be given. Assemblers are not usually provided with computers, and have to be purchased separately.

1.9   FURTHER READING

The description of computer architecture in this chapter has, of necessity, been rather brief. More detailed discussions can be found in the following books also published by Bernard Babani (publishing) Ltd:

Book No. BP72 – A Microprocessor Primer
Book No. BP78 – Practical Computer Experiments
Book No. BP66 – Beginners Guide to Microprocessors
Book No. BP77 – Elements of Electronics - Book 4,
                          Microprocessing Systems and Circuits

Chapter Two

Z-80 ARCHITECTURE

2.1 INTRODUCTION

This chapter introduces the Z-80 microprocessor, describing its architecture and role in the construction of a microcomputer. The Z-80, like all microprocessors, is the CPU of a perfectly conventional computer, and needs store and I/O before it can be useful. The connection of these items is discussed. This chapter is therefore concerned with equipment. Chapter 3 will describe the Z-80 instruction set and will be concerned with software.

2.2 GENERAL ARCHITECTURE

2.2.1 The Z-80 registers

The Z-80 can be represented by the block diagram of Fig.2.1 which is very similar to the generalised CPU diagram of Fig.1.5 in Chapter 1. The Z-80 is an 8 bit microprocessor, and can address 64K of store. It therefore utilises an 8 bit data bus and a 16 bit address bus. There are also 13 control signals in the control bus.

The registers, PC, instruction decode, ALU and control fulfill the same functions as described for Fig.1.5. The instruction register simply holds the instruction currently being obeyed.

The user of the Z-80 is interested in the block labelled "registers". This is shown expanded on Fig.2.2. The Z-80 has an impressive array of registers, 17 8 bit registers, one 7 bit register and 4 16 bit registers. The first point of note is that these registers are in three groups, main register set, alternate register set, and special purpose.

The main register set and alternate register set are identical. The programmer chooses which set he wishes to work with at

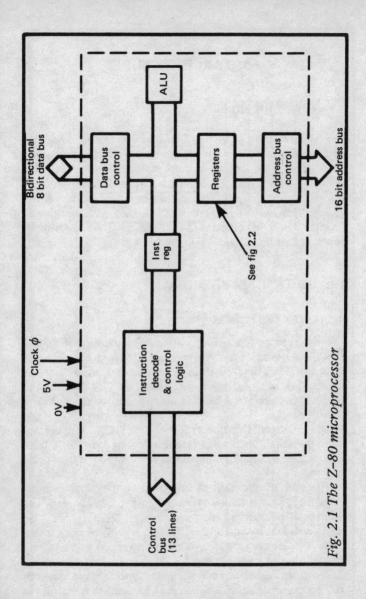

Fig. 2.1 The Z-80 microprocessor

18

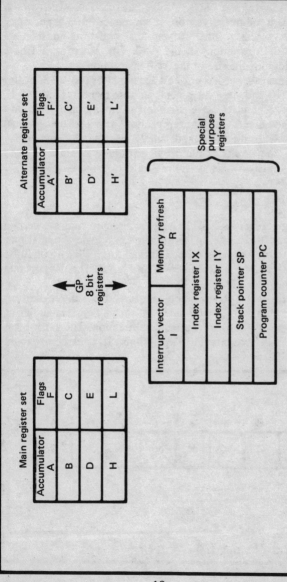

Fig. 2.2 The Z-80 registers

any time by the use of "Exchange" instructions which switch sets. This is, admittedly, a bit of a nuisance but it is necessary to allow access to the 16 registers whilst minimising the number of instructions in the Z-80. Full access would have nearly doubled the size of the Z-80 instruction set.

Each register set has an 8 bit accumulator (A), an 8 bit flag register (F) and six 8 bit general purpose registers (B,C,D,E,H, L). The accumulators are used for arithmetic and logic purposes; the other 6 G.P. registers cannot (with a few exceptions) be used with the ALU and simply provide fast temporary storage. The results of almost all arithmetic operations go to the accumulators.

2.2.2   Flag Registers (F)

The flag registers are 8 bit registers used to indicate certain conditions that arise in arithmetic and logical operations. These are used as tests for conditional jumps. Each condition is represented by a bit, as shown on Fig.2.3. The flags operate as below.

The carry flag (C) is simply the carry from the highest bit of the accumulator, and is set if a "carry" is generated during an add, or a "borrow" during a subtraction. The carry bit is also altered by some shift operations. If twos complement

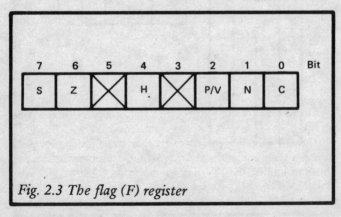

Fig. 2.3 The flag (F) register

20

arithmetic (see Appendix A) is being used, the carry does not necessarily indicate if an overflow has occurred. The P/V flag should be used for this purpose.

The zero flag (Z) is set when the last instruction affecting the flags resulted in zero contents of the accumulator. Any non zero contents resets the flag.

The sign flag (S) is used with twos complement arithmetic, and simply indicates if the accumulator is positive (S=0) or negative (S=1), because bit 7 of an 8 bit twos complement number indicates the sign. The S flag is simply a copy of bit 7. Note that zero is a positive number.

The parity/overflow flag (P/V) serves two purposes. After a logical operation (AND, OR, Exclusive OR) the flag indicates the parity of the result, being set for an even parity and reset for an odd parity. The second use requires a little more explanation. If twos complement arithmetic is being used, an 8 bit word represents a *SIGNED* number in the range -128 to $+127$. Bit 7 indicates the sign, being 0 for positive numbers and 1 for negative numbers. With twos complement arithmetic, the carry bit does not reliably indicate if an overflow has occurred. Consider the two examples below:

$$
\begin{array}{rcl}
123 & = & 0111\ 1011 \\
+\ 106 & = & \underline{0110\ 1010} \\
C=0 & & 1110\ 0101 \quad = \quad -91
\end{array}
$$

The result is an incorrect negative number, but the carry bit has not been set.

$$
\begin{array}{rcl}
-\ 5 & & 1111\ 1011 \\
-\ 16 & & \underline{1111\ 0000} \\
C=1 & & 1110\ 1011 \quad = \quad -21
\end{array}
$$

In this case, the result is correct, but the carry bit has been set.

The P/V flag indicates correctly if an overflow has occurred during a twos complement arithmetical operation. In the two above examples, the P/V flag would be set for the first (overflow has occurred) and reset for the second (overflow has not occurred). It follows that the carry flag is used for unsigned 8 bit arithmetic, and the P/V flag for signed twos complement arithmetic.

The C, Z, S, P/V flags are used with conditional jumps and conditional subroutine calls. The Z-80 uses the following conditions:

Carry	C = 1
Non Carry	C = 0
Zero	Z = 1
Non Zero	Z = 0
Parity Even	P/V = 1
Parity Odd	P/V = 0
Sign Negative	S = 1
Sign Positive	S = 0

The four flags above can be used directly for conditional jumps. There are also two flags which are used by the internal logic of the Z-80 when BCD operations are being performed. These cannot be used directly in conditional jumps, but can be accessed as any other bit in any other register.

The first of these flags is the half carry (H) used to indicate the BCD carry or borrow result from the least significant four bits of the accumulator. This flag is used by the Decimal Adjust instruction, described later.

The Add/Subtract flag (N) indicates if the last instruction was an addition or subtraction. The algorithm used by the Decimal Adjust instruction is different for addition or subtraction, the correct algorithm being selected by the N flag.

The flags are not altered by all instructions. In general, the flags are altered by all arithmetical and logical operations. Load instructions (store reads and writes and inter register transfers) leave the flags unaffected.

2.2.3 General Purpose Registers (B, C, D, E, H, L)

Each register set has six general purpose registers (B, C, D, E, H, L). These provide fast temporary storage. They can also be grouped as 16 bit register pairs (BC, DE, HL) providing 16 bit arithmetic facilities and a powerful method of addressing known as register indirect (to be described later in section 3.3.6).

2.2.4 Special Purpose Registers (I, R, PC, IX, IY, SP)

There are six special purpose registers, denoted I, R, PC, IX, IY, SP. Although these are usually dedicated to one task they can, in general, be accessed like any other register.

PC is the 16 bit program counter, operating exactly as described in Chapter 1. A 16 bit program counter is necessary to address 64K of store.

IX and IY are two 16 bit registers used in a useful method of addressing the store known as Indexed Addressing. This is described further in section 3.3.7.

SP stands for Stack Pointer, and is another 16 bit register. To understand the use of the stack pointer we must first describe the concept of the "stack". We described the idea of subroutines in the previous chapter. When a subroutine is called, we must somehow save the contents of the PC, and substitute the address of the subroutine. At the end of the subroutine we must reinstate the PC to its original value.

To achieve this, an area of store is designated to hold PC addresses during subroutine calls. Normally the stack starts at the top of the store and comes down. The SP holds the current position of the end of the stack. Because addresses are 16 bits, each address takes two store locations on the stack.

The operation of the stack is best demonstrated by an example. Let us assume we are obeying the instruction at location 0C50, and it is a call to a subroutine at 1D00. The stack pointer is currently at 2F05, indicating that the stack ends at 2F05. The sequence below is then followed:

i. PC contents are put into 2F05 and 2F04. (i.e. the address of the subroutine call is put onto the stack)
ii. PC contents are replaced by 1D00 (the address of the subroutine)
iii. The SP is decremented to 2F03 (to allow for nesting of subroutines. The stack can be of any length)
iv. The subroutine is obeyed.

23

At the end of the subroutine, a return instruction initiates the following sequence:

i. The SP is incremented and used to bring a 16 bit number back from the stack to the PC. If addresses have been placed and read from the stack in sequence, this will bring 0C50 back to the PC.

ii. The PC is incremented to step onto the instruction following the subroutine call.

iii. The main program continues.

Putting an address onto the stack is known as a PUSH. Getting an address from the stack is known as a PULL. The important point to remember about a stack is Last In, First Out.

The stack can also be used to store data from register pairs. This must be done with care, as the programmer must ensure that the data comes off the stack in the expected order. The sequence in Fig.2.4 will *NOT* work as expected because the data brought to BC will be the last data pushed onto the stack; the address of the instruction calling the subroutine call. The address replaced in the PC by the return instruction will be the contents of BC pushed onto the stack earlier. Remember, Last In, First Out.

The two final registers are denoted I (for interrupt) and R (for refresh). The I register is known as the Interrupt Page Address Register, and is used when the Z-80 is controlling external devices. There is a vast difference in speed between computers and peripheral devices, which is reconciled by a technique known as Interrupts. This will be described in detail in Chapter 6, but for the present an interrupt can best be considered as a subroutine call initiated by an external device. The device supplies the low byte of the subroutine address, the I register supplies the high byte.

The 7 bit R register is used when the store is constructed with dynamic memory ICs. (Such as the popular 4116). These store the data as charges on capacitors (see Fig.2.5) which have to be refreshed every few milliseconds. Normally this refreshing is performed by external logic which grabs control of the highway at regular intervals to perform the refresh operation. The

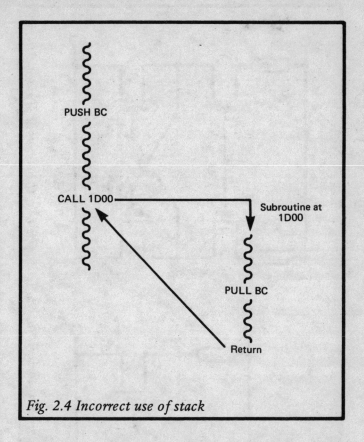

PUSH BC

CALL 1D00 ——————————┐
                     │ Subroutine at
                     │   1D00
                     ↓

                   PULL BC

                   Return

Fig. 2.4 Incorrect use of stack

Z-80 is unique amongst micros in containing its own refresh logic. The R register contains the current refresh address. The contents of the R register are placed on the lower 7 bits of the address bus along with a refresh signal on the control bus when the bus is free. After each refresh the R register is automatically incremented. The whole refresh operation is totally invisible to the user.

Chapter 3 will describe how data is moved and manipulated in the registers and store.

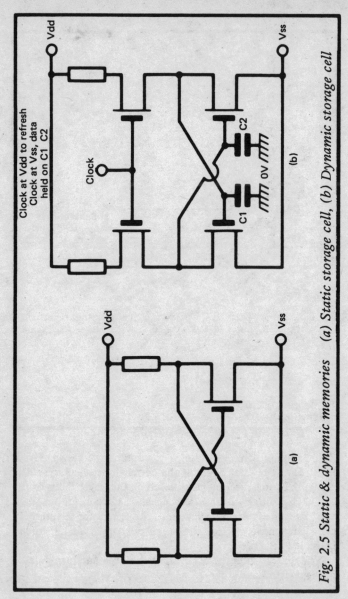

Fig. 2.5 Static & dynamic memories   (a) Static storage cell, (b) Dynamic storage cell

26

2.3   EXTERNAL CONNECTIONS

A typical small Z-80 system is shown on Fig.2.6. This should be compared with Fig.1.2. The Z-80 itself is a standard 40 pin dual in line IC with connections shown on Fig.2.7. It will be seen that the connections form the address bus, data bus and control bus described earlier.

2.3.1   Address Bus

The address bus is A0—A15, A0 being the least significant bit and A15 the most significant bit. The address bus can address up to 64K of store. The least significant 8 bits (A0 – A7) are also used to address I/O ports, allowing up to 256 I/O addresses. The address highway conveys the address in "true" form.

2.3.2   Data Bus

The data bus is D0 – D7, D0 being the least significant bit. This is a bidirectional highway, conveying data between store, I/O ports and the Z-80.

2.3.3   Control Bus Outputs

The control bus contains 13 signals; 8 outputs and 5 inputs. The first of these is $\overline{RD}$, memory read. This indicates that the CPU wants to read data from a memory location or I/O port. The signal is active low, and is present whilst the address bus holds a valid address. $\overline{RD}$ is used by the addressed location or port to gate data onto the data bus.

$\overline{WR}$, write, indicates that the CPU requires to send data to a store location or I/O port. The signal is active low, and is present whilst the address bus holds a valid address and the data bus valid data. $\overline{WR}$ and $\overline{RD}$ are effectively strobe signals similar to those on Fig.1.3.

$\overline{MREQ}$, memory request, is an active low signal indicating that the address bus holds a valid address. $\overline{MREQ}$ appears in conjunction with $\overline{RD}$ or $\overline{WR}$.

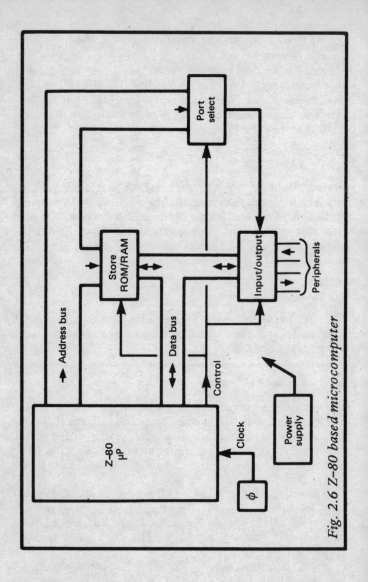

Fig. 2.6 Z-80 based microcomputer

28

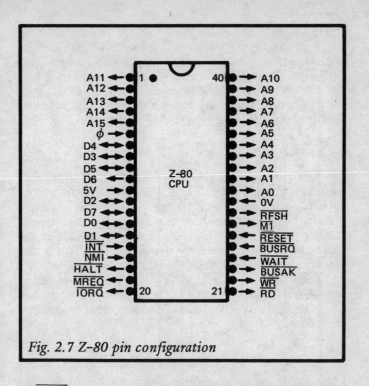

Fig. 2.7 Z–80 pin configuration

$\overline{\text{IORQ}}$ denotes input/output. This active low signal indicates that the address on A0 — A7 is the address of an I/O port, and an input/output transfer is to be performed. $\overline{\text{IORQ}}$ allows memory locations and I/O ports to share the same address. $\overline{\text{IORQ}}$ appears with $\overline{\text{RD}}$ or $\overline{\text{WR}}$ to indicate if data is to be input or output. $\overline{\text{IORQ}}$ is also used in the timing of interrupts, to be described later in section 6.4.

$\overline{\text{RFSH}}$ stands for refresh and is an active low signal indicating that A0 — A6 contain an address that can be used to refresh dynamic memories. $\overline{\text{MREQ}}$ appears with $\overline{\text{RFSH}}$.

$\overline{\text{HALT}}$ indicates simply that the CPU has halted following a HALT instruction. The signal is active low. The memory refresh for dynamic memories continues even though the processor is halted.

$\overline{M1}$ stands for machine cycle one. It was explained in Chapter 1 that obeying an instruction consists of a fetch of the instruction from the store followed by a data read and/or a data write. In the Z-80 the instruction fetch is known as M1, the memory read as M2 and the memory write as M3. $\overline{M1}$ is an active low signal indicating that the CPU is in the M1 state. The signal is used in timing some I/O operations.

2.3.4 Control Bus Inputs

The first control input is the $\overline{WAIT}$ signal. The Z-80 is faster than some memory and I/O control devices, particularly when a 4MHz clock is used. The $\overline{WAIT}$ signal is used by an addressed memory or I/O port to indicate that the required data transfer can not yet take place. On receipt of a $\overline{WAIT}$ signal the CPU simply pauses. The $\overline{WAIT}$ signal is active low. During the $\overline{WAIT}$ state the memory refresh is not maintained.

$\overline{RESET}$ is used to force the CPU to a known state, and is normally used at power up or to regain control if a program has gone off the rails. The $\overline{RESET}$ input is active low and has the following effects.

    i. PC, I and R are reset to zero
   ii. Interrupts are disabled and interrupt Mode 0 is set.

Interrupts are described later in section 6.4. Resetting the PC has the effect of an unconditional jump to location zero.

$\overline{INT}$ is also an interrupt request from an external device. A "low" on this line initiates the interrupt sequence.

$\overline{NMI}$ is also an interrupt request, but is a higher priority than $\overline{INT}$. The CPU can ignore the $\overline{INT}$ signal, but $\overline{NMI}$, standing for Non Maskable Interrupt, is always recognised. $\overline{NMI}$ effects a subroutine call to location Hex 66. The $\overline{NMI}$ is negative edge triggered.

2.3.5 Bus Control

In large systems, the address data and control buses can be shared with another CPU or devices such as disc controllers which require access to the memory without the CPU. Under these circumstances, the CPU is occasionally required to release the buses for use by the other devices requesting access. This is achieved by two signals on the control bus.

BUSRQ (Bus request) is an input from an external device requesting control of the buses. The signal is active low. On receipt of $\overline{BUSRQ}$ the Z-80 sets all its bus signals to a high impedance state, allowing the requesting device to use the buses. The Z-80 then takes $\overline{BUSAK}$ to a 'low' to indicate that the requesting device can use the buses. Whilst the Z-80 has released the buses, memory refreshing obviously ceases.

2.3.6 Other Signals

The Z-80 needs a 5 volt supply (Vcc and 0V) and a clock (ϕ). The clock is usually provided by a simple crystal oscillator and can be 1, 2, or 4MHz dependent on the version of Z-80 and the application.

2.4 BUS TIMING

The actual timing of the bus signals is usually of little concern to the amateur. Fig. 2.8 and 2.9 show, somewhat simplified, the timing of a memory read and a memory write operation.

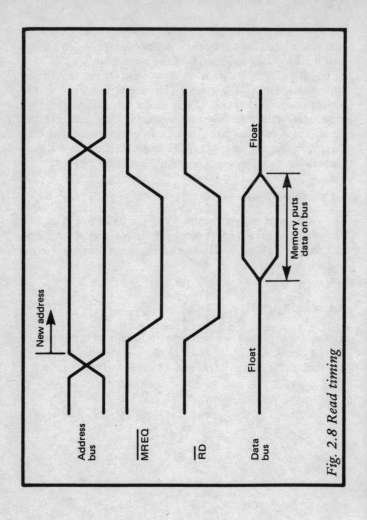

Fig. 2.8 Read timing

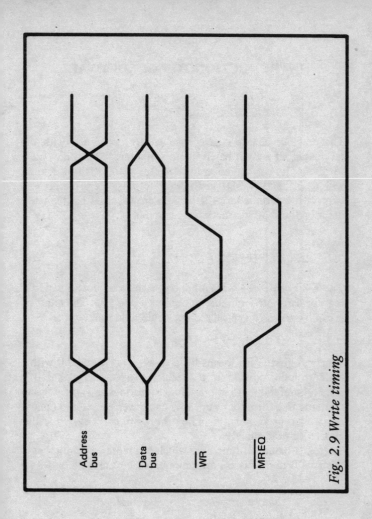

Address
bus

Data
bus

$\overline{WR}$

$\overline{MREQ}$

Fig. 2.9 Write timing

33

Chapter Three

INTRODUCTION TO Z-80 SOFTWARE

3.1 INTRODUCTION

The previous chapters have been largely concerned with the mechanics of a Z-80 based microcomputer. We can now start to discuss how programs are written for the Z-80. This chapter will describe the Z-80 instruction set in general terms and explain the various terms used in later sections. Chapter 4 will describe the Z-80 instruction set in detail.

3.2 HEX REPRESENTATION

The Z-80 deals with 8 bit numbers; each store location and GP register can hold a number in the range 0 to 255. The numbers are in binary, so a typical register could hold the number

$$1010 \quad 0111$$

which at first sight, means little to anyone. We could, with a little trouble, convert it to decimal (167 actually) but it is usually preferable to represent a store location and register contents in a form that can easily be converted back to binary. Most microprocessors, including the Z-80, use a system called Hex (for hexadecimal).

Hex is based on four bits, which can represent a number in the rage 0 to 15. These are represented by the symbols 0 to 9 followed by A to F

Binary	Hex	Decimal
0000	0	0
0001	1	1
0010	2	2
0011	3	3
0100	4	4
0101	5	5

Binary	Hex	Decimal
0 1 1 0	6	6
0 1 1 1	7	7
1 0 0 0	8	8
1 0 0 1	9	9
1 0 1 0	A	10
1 0 1 1	B	11
1 1 0 0	C	12
1 1 0 1	D	13
1 1 1 0	E	14
1 1 1 1	F	15

To represent a binary number in Hex, you simply split it into 4 bit chunks, and put the Hex equivalent underneath. For example:

```
              1 0 1 0 0 1 1 1
becomes     1 0 1 0         0 1 1 1
giving        A               7
```

So the binary word 1 0 1 0 0 1 1 1 is A7 in Hex.

```
Another example     0 1 0 0 1 1 0 0
becomes          0 1 0 0         1 1 0 0
giving             4               C
```

It is equally easy to go from Hex to binary. The four bit pattern for the Hex number is simply written underneath. For example D2 becomes

```
         D         2
       1 1 0 1   0 0 1 0
```

giving 1 1 0 1 0 0 1 0 as the binary equivalent of Hex D2.

```
Another example     F         A
gives             1 1 1 1   1 0 1 0
```

The Z-80 instruction set is given in Chapter 4 in Hex form. 8A, for example, is the instruction that will make the Z-80 add the contents of register D to the Accumulator.

Hex representation can also be used on 16 bit numbers such as store addresses), for example:

35

	1 1 1 0	0 1 0 1	1 0 1 0	1 0 0 1
becomes	E	5	A	9

and in reverse

	0	C	5	7
becomes	0 0 0 0	1 1 0 0	0 1 0 1	0 1 1 1

Store addresses in Z-80 microcomputers are usually given in Hex.

Hex can be a bit daunting at first, but it should be remembered that it is just a convenient shorthand method of representing binary numbers. With a little practice, binary to Hex and Hex to binary becomes second nature.

3.3 ADDRESS MODES

3.3.1 Introduction

An instruction will normally involve data in one or two locations or registers. This data will be moved or manipulated in some form (e.g. Add Subtract, etc.). An instruction therefore must usually specify two things:

  i. What is to be done (e.g. move, add, subtract)
  ii. Where the data is to be found (e.g. Register A, location 3220)

In older computers, which used a 16 bit word length, it was common to allocate the op code (specifying what is to be done) to the top few bits, and the address of the data to the remainder of the word as shown on Fig.3.1. This is known as direct addressing, because the number representing the instruction directly indicates the store location where the data is to be found or stored.

There is a problem, however, with all 8 bit microprocessors. An 8 bit word can represent a number in the range of $0 - 255$. The Z-80 has 158 different instructions, so it will take all 8 bits of a microprocessor word simply to specify the Op Code. To specify a 64K address requires an additional 16 bits.

Obviously direct addressing cannot be used, at least not in the simple form of Fig.3.1. All 8 bit microprocessors use a collection of ingenious methods called address modes to address the store.

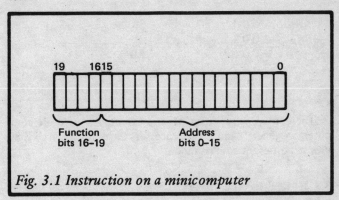

Fig. 3.1 Instruction on a minicomputer

The first, slightly confusing, idea is the use of different lengths of instruction. A Z-80 instruction can be 8, 16, 24 or 32 bits in length (occupying respectively 1, 2, 3 and 4 store locations). The first location will always be an Op Code. Subsequent locations define where the data is to be found. The following are typical Hex coded Z-80 instructions:

7A	Move the contents of register D to the accumulator
06 FF	Put the Hex value FF into Register B
C3 50 0C	Jump to location 0C50
ED 43 FE IF	Store the 16 bit number in Register Pair BC to store locations IF FE and IF FF

In each case the first 8 bits define the Op Code (7A, 06, C3, ED). In the latter case the full Op Code actually occupies two locations (ED 43) but the ED portion specifies the form of the instruction, and 43 the register pair.

If the 4 instructions above were stored from location Hex 1000 we would have:

37

Location	Contents
1 0 0 0	7A
1 0 0 1	06
1 0 0 2	FF
1 0 0 3	C3
1 0 0 4	50
1 0 0 5	0C
1 0 0 6	ED
1 0 0 7	43
1 0 0 8	FE
1 0 0 9	IF

There are many different address modes used in computers in general, and microprocessors in particular. The Z-80 uses ten different address modes.

3.3.2 Register Addressing

Many instructions in the Z-80 set only involve data held in the registers. Examples are "move the contents of Register B to Register A" or "Move the contents of Register D to Register C". These, and similar instructions are said to use Register Addressing. Most of these instructions are a single byte (8 bits) in length and occupy one location. The Op Code for "Move the contents of Register B to Register A" is the single byte instruction 78.

3.3.3 Immediate Addressing

Immediate addressing is used where the data to be manipulated is fixed. For example "Load Register B with 42" or "Add 7 to Register A". These instructions take the form:

> Op Code   One or two bytes
> Data

"Add 7 to Register A" is actually C6 07, C6 being the Op Code and 07 the data.

3.3.4 Extended Addressing

Extended addressing is almost identical to direct addressing described earlier. The store address for the data is given in full 16 bits in the instruction. Examples are "Move the contents of store location 0C50 to Register A" or "Call the subroutine at location 1DF5". The address occupies two locations in the instruction, and the Op Code one or two locations. Extended Address instructions therefore occupy three or four locations:

Op Code	One or two bytes
Address Bottom	8 bits
Address Top	8 bits

The Z-80 code for "Call the subroutine at location 1DF5" is CD F5 1D. CD is the Op Code and F5 1D indicates the address 1DF5. It might seem more logical to have the instruction written CD 1D F5, but consider how the instruction is stored:

Location	Contents	
N	CD	
N + 1	F5	address low byte) Address 1DF5
N + 2	1D	address high byte)

The address is stored in two locations, N + 1, N + 2. The low byte of the address is simply stored in the low byte of the instruction (N + 1) and the high byte of the address in the high byte of the instruction (N + 2).

3.3.5 Immediate Extended Addressing

This addressing mode is used with 16 bit data in two successive store locations, register pairs (BC, DE, HL) and the index registers. For example, we could have "Load register pair BC with 0C50". An immediate extended instruction takes the form of a three of four location instructions:

> Op Code (one or two bytes)
> Data Low Byte
> Data High Byte

"Load register BC with 0C50" is actually 01 50 0C with 01 the Op Code and 0C50 the data. As with extended Addressing, it might be thought more logical to have coded this 01 0C 50, but in fact the low byte of the data goes to the low byte of the instruction.

When register pairs are used, high and low bytes are allocated

High	Low
B	C
D	E
H	L

3.3.6   Register Indirect Addressing

A register pair, being 16 bits in length, can hold a 16 bit address and therefore can be used to indicate a store location. In register indirect addressing a register pair is used to indicate the store location for the data. An example would be "Store the contents of register A in store location whose address is to be found in register pair BC". Suppose A contains 2D (in Hex) and BC contains 1C72 (B is high byte, C is low byte). The number 2D would be stored in location 1C72. This is summarised by Fig.3.2.

Because the address is provided by a register pair, a register direct instruction consists only of an Op Code one or two bytes in length. The code for "Store the contents of A in the store location whose address is to be found in register pair BC" is actually 02.

3.3.7   Indexed Addressing

Indexed addressing is a special form of register indirect addressing that is particularly useful where tables of data held in successive store locations have to be processed. The Z-80 has two index registers, each 16 bits in length, which provide a *base* 16 bit address. The instruction contains a twos complement offset known as the displacement (in the range −127 to +128) which is added to the base address in an index register

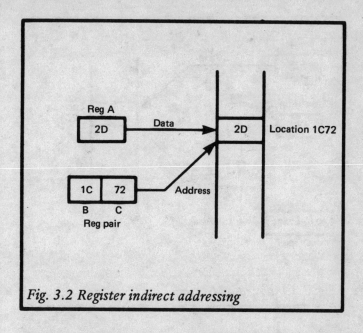

Fig. 3.2 Register indirect addressing

to give the address to be used for the data. For example, we could have "Store register B, index addressed with IX, displacement 05". Let us assume register B contains FE, index register X contains 2D10. The instruction would store FE in location 2D15.

An index address instruction always occupies three locations and consists of a 2 byte Op Code and a 1 Byte displacement:

> Op Code   (two bytes)
> Displacement   (one byte)

The coding for "Store register B, index addresses with IX, displace 05" is actually DD 70 05. DD 70 is the Op code, 05 the displacement. (See Fig. 3.3)

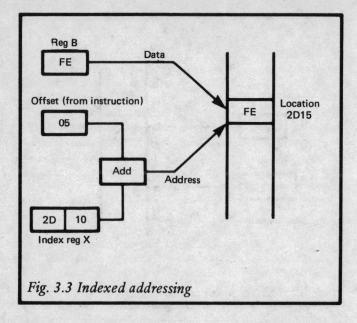

Fig. 3.3 Indexed addressing

3.3.8 Relative Addressing

Relative addressing is used only for jumps in the Z-80. The current instruction address is used as a base address, and the instruction contains a twos complement displacement (in the range −128 to +127) to give the jump destination. In the Z-80, slightly confusingly the base address is actually the current location +2. A typical relative addressed instruction is "Jump relative +16" (remember, the displacement 16 is Hex). If we were at location 0C50, the base address is 0C52 and we would jump to the instruction at 0C68. Note that because a twos complement displacement is used we can jump both forward and backward from the current location. All relative addressed instructions use two locations, one for the Op Code and one for the displacement:

Op Code	One byte
Displacement	One byte

The code for "Jump Relative +16" is 18 16, with 18 the Op Code and 16 the displacement.

Relative addressing is very useful. Apart from being a neat and compact way of writing jumps, it allows programs to be written that can be placed anywhere in the store. These are known as relocatable programs. Usually a programmer builds up a library of relocatable subroutines for common items such as multiplication, division, outputs to printers etc. which can be plugged into each new program as needed. The disadvantage of relative addressing is the tedious recalculation of the displacements if debugging requires the insertion or removal of instructions.

3.3.9 Modified Page Zero Addressing

There are 8 page zero addressed instructions. All are subroutine calls known as restarts to addresses below Hex 100. All consist of a single byte Op Code. DF, for example, is "Call subroutine at location Hex 18". The 8 Restart subroutine calls are a very compact way of calling frequently used subroutines.

3.3.10 Implied Addressing

Some instructions inherently imply where the data is to be found. Exchange instructions (which switch register sets) are typical implied instructions.

3.3.11 Bit Addressing

In data processing and control engineering, single bits in an 8 bit word are used to indicate an event being present or not. A bit could be used, for example, to represent a limit switch being open or closed. In file applications a bit could represent the sex of a person; '1' for male, '0' for female.

The Z-80 has a comprehensive range of bit addressed instructions that allow a single bit in a register or store location to be set, reset or tested (via the flag register, F).

3.3.12 General Observations

We have described ten different address modes, and it is quite possible that the reader is feeling a bit punchdrunk. For completeness, we will list them:

i. Register Addressing
ii. Immediate Addressing
iii. Extended Addressing
iv. Immediate Extended Addressing
v. Register Indirect Addressing
vi. Indexed Addressing
vii. Relative Addressing
viii. Modified Page Zero Addressing
ix. Implied Addressing
x. Bit Addressing

It is worth noting that almost any program can be written using only the first four modes, and most programs using the first three. The resulting program will certainly not be elegant, fast, or short, but it will work. It is suggested that the would-be programmer simply masters the first three modes, and writes simple programs using them until he (or she) is reasonably competent. At that point mastery of the remainder of the addressing modes should be quite easy, and the programmer can produce more elegant programs.

Not every addressing mode is available on every instruction, so the tables in Chapter 4 should be consulted until the reader is familiar with the Z-80 instruction set.

3.4 INSTRUCTION TYPES

3.4.1 Introduction

Chapter 4 gives the complete Z-80 instruction set in tabular form. This section describes the types of instruction available in a less formal manner. There are just 8 groups of instruction in the Z-80:

i. Loads
ii. Arithmetic and Logic
iii. Jumps and Subroutine calls
iv. Shifts
v. Block Transfers
vi. Bit Manipulation
vii. Input/Output
viii. Control

These 8 groups of instructions are combined with the addressing modes described in section 3.3 to give the 158 different instruction types available on the Z-80.

3.4.2 Load Instructions

In Chapter 1 we described the read and write instructions which moved data between registers and the store. In the Z-80, read and write operations and data movements between individual registers are collectively known as "Loads". The following are therefore examples of "Load instructions".

Store the data from register A into store location 0C50.
Read the data from store location 12FA to register A.
Store the data from register B into the store location whose address is held in register pair HL.
Move the data in register D to register C.

3.4.3 Arithmetic and Logic Instructions

Almost all Z-80 arithmetic instructions are performed on data in Register A (the accumulator) and data in a store or another register. The result invariably goes to register A. The Z-80 can perform the following 8 bit operations:

i. Add
ii. Add with Carry (ADC)
iii. Subtract
iv. Sub with Carry (SBC)
v. AND

45

vi. Exclusive OR (XOR)
vii. Compare (CP)
viii. Increment
ix. Decrement

Add and Subtract with carry include the carry flag in the operation. Suppose we obey "Add register B to Register A with carry", and register A contains 0101 1010 (5A in Hex), register B contains 0010 0011 (23 in Hex) with the carry flag set we would get:

```
0101  1010          A
0010  0011          B
            1       Carry flag
_____
0111  1110          Result to A
```

If the carry flag is not set we would get:

```
0101  1010          A
0010  0011          B
            0       Carry flag
_____
0111  1101          Result to A
```

Incorporating the carry flag into the operation simplifies the writing of the programs with 16 bit numbers.

The simple Add and Subtract instructions ignore the state of the carry flag, and just operate on the two 8 bit words.

All arithmetic operations set (or reset) the S, Z, H, V, N, C flags according to the result of the operations. The P/V flag works on the overflow.

The logical operations AND, OR and XOR are performed bit by bit between data in register A and data in another register, Suppose we have:

```
1010  0101          Register A   (A5 in Hex)
1001  1101          Register B   (9D in Hex)
```

the result of AND is   1000 0101 (85 in Hex)
the result of OR is   1011 1101 (BD in Hex)
the result of XOR is   0011 1000 (38 in Hex)

In all three operations the result goes to register A, and the

S, Z and P/V flags are set or reset according to the result. The P/V flag works on the parity of the result.

The compare operations is used to compare the data in register A with some other specified data. The operations does not affect the data itself, but sets (or resets) the S, Z, H, V and C flags according to the result (Contents A − Specified Data). If we ask for the instruction Compare Register A, Register B for the data below the flags set would be:

A	B	Flags	Comments
06	07	SHNC	A < B
07	06	N	A > B
06	06	ZN	A = B

Care should be taken if one of the numbers is using bit 8 as a sign bit e.g.

A	B	Flags
FF	01	SN
01	FF	HNC

Usually the compare instruction is used to test for equality (e.g. the Z flag set) and is invariably followed by a conditional jump or subroutine call on the state of the Z flag.

Increment and Decrement are useful instructions. Increment takes some specified data, adds '1' to it and places the result back again. Decrement operates in a similar manner except that '1' is subtracted. The data can be obtained from any register or (using register indirect or indexed addressing) any store location. The following are typical increment instructions:

Add 1 to Register C
Add 1 to the contents of the store location whose address is in HL

The following are typical decrement instructions:

Subtract 1 from Register E
Subtract 1 from the contents of the store location (index register X + 5)

Note that unlike all other arithmetic operations, the result goes back to the source of the data and *NOT* to register A. Increment and decrement instructions are a convenient way of counting events.

3.4.4 Jumps and Subroutine Calls

The idea of jump instructions and subroutine calls was introduced in Chapter 1. The Z-80 has a very useful range of conditional jumps and subroutine calls and returns. The conditions tested are based on the flags in the F register and are:

Carry Set, Carry Not Set, Accumulator Zero, Accumulator Non Zero, Parity Even, Parity Odd, Sign Negative, Sign Positive.

The majority of these instructions use extended addressing (e.g. CC 70 0F, call subroutine starting at location 0F 70 if the accumulator is zero). There are also a few jump instructions using relative addressing and three unconditional jump instructions using register indirect addressing.

Subroutine calls use the stack pointer to store the current value of the program counter, and return instructions reinstate the value from the stack back to the program counter at the end of the subroutine. The stack operation was described in section 2.2.4.

3.4.5 Rotates and Shifts

A shift instruction simply moves the bit pattern in a register one place to the left or right. Suppose we had

$$1 0 1 0 \quad 0 1 1 1 \qquad \text{(A7 in Hex)}$$

A simple shift to the left would give

$$0 1 0 0 \quad 1 1 1 0 \qquad \text{(4E in Hex)}$$

A simple shift to the right would give

$$0 1 0 1 \quad 0 0 1 1 \qquad \text{(53 in Hex)}$$

In each case the bit pushed off the end is "lost", and a zero

48

placed at the other end. These are known as a logical shift.

Consider the simple bit pattern 0101, which is five in decimal. If the pattern is shifted one place to the left (called shifting up) we get 1010 which is ten in decimal. A shift up is equivalent to multiplying by two providing the top bit is not shifted off the end.

Similarly, if we have the bit pattern 1100, which is twelve in decimal and shift it one place to the right (called shifting down) we get 0110 which is six in decimal. A shift down is equivalent to a division by two.

A simple shift will, however, give the wrong result on signed number. If twos complement representation is used, bit 7 represents the sign, being a '1' for negative numbers and '0' for positive numbers. We thus have:

1 1 1 1	1 0 0 0	(−8 decimal)
1 1 1 1	1 1 0 0	(−4 decimal)
1 1 1 1	1 1 1 0	(−2 decimal)
1 1 1 1	1 1 1 1	(−1 decimal)

Although we are dividing by two by shifting to the right, it is not a simple shift because the sign bit must be maintained. This is known as an arithmetic shift, and can be summarised by Fig. 3.4.

Rotate instructions are very similar to shifts. In a rotate instruction the 'lost' bit is simply fed into the opposite end of the register as shown on Fig.3.5. The effect of successive rotate rights would therefore be:

start	0 1 1 0	0 1 0 1
rotate right	1 0 1 1	0 0 1 0
rotate right	0 1 0 1	1 0 0 1
rotate right	1 0 1 0	1 1 0 0
etc.		

The Z-80 has seven types of rotate and shift instructions. These all incorporate the carry flag as shown on Fig.3.6. These operations can be performed on every general purpose register and (using register indirect or indexed addressing) on store contents.

Shift instructions are the basis for writing multiplication

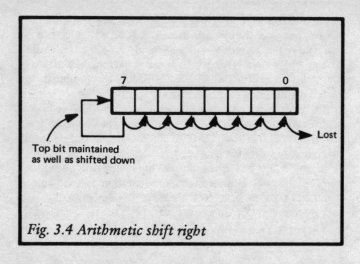

Fig. 3.4 Arithmetic shift right

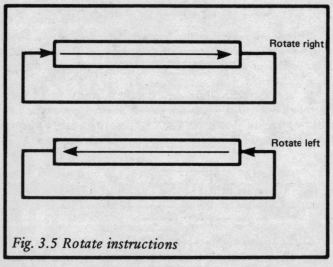

Fig. 3.5 Rotate instructions

and division routines, and both shifts and rotates are widely used where individual bits are used to represent data in control applications or data processing as described in section 3.3.11.

50

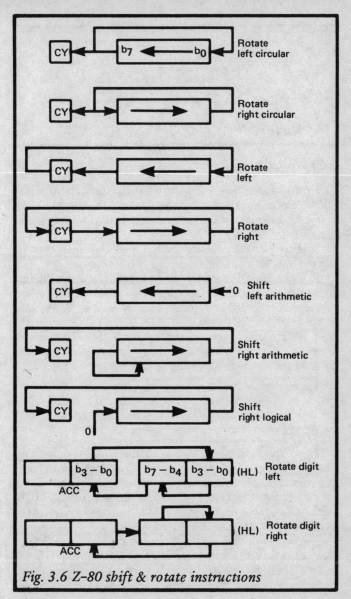

Fig. 3.6 Z–80 shift & rotate instructions

51

'0' = zero
CY = carry flag
(HL) = store location whose
address is held in HL
ACC = register A (i.e. Accumulator)

Fig. 3.6 (b)

3.4.6 Block Transfer

The Z-80 has a unique set of block transfer instructions. These allow "blocks" of data to be moved around the store with just a few instructions. These instructions all involve the register pairs HL, DE, BC.

Register pair HL contains the 16 bit address where the first item of data is to be found.

Register pair DE contains the 16 bit address where the first item is to be stored.

Register pair BC is a 16 bit counter used to define how many words are to be moved.

If HL contained, say, 0C50, DE, 2000 and BC 100, a block transfer instruction would move 100 (Hex) words from 0C50 to 2000 and succeeding locations as summarised on Fig.3.7.

The contents of 0C50 would go to 2000
                0C51   to 2001
                0C52   to 2002 and so on for 100
locations.

There are four block transfer instructions. The first two operate as above, and are known as "load increment repeat, (LDIR)" and "load decrement repeat, (LDDR)". These operate as above, except LDIR works up the store and LDDR works down the store allowing data to be transferred between overlapping locations as shown on Fig.3.8.

The two remaining block transfer instructions transfer one word each time the instruction is obeyed, but set up HL, DE and BC ready for the next transfer. These allow other instructions to be incorporated in the block transfer operation. An

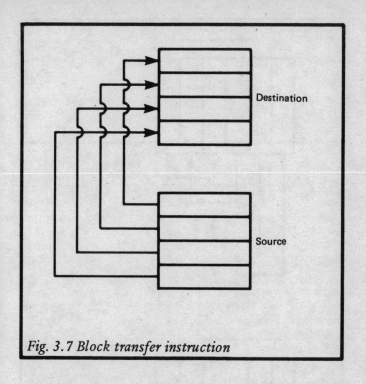

Fig. 3.7 Block transfer instruction

example is shown on Fig.3.9 which is a flow chart for an operation which transfers a block of data, terminating either when the full block is transferred or a word containing "FF" (Hex) is found. As before, an incrementing and decrementing instruction is provided to allow data to be transferred between overlapping locations. The instructions are known as "Load decrement (LDD)" and "Load increment (LDI)".

The Z-80 also has four powerful block search instructions which allow an area of store to be compared with the accumulator contents. HL contains the start address, and BC is a counter indicating the number of locations to be searched. As before, the search can be conducted up or down the store, and can be conducted one word at a time (compare increment (CPI) and compare decrement (CPD)) or at one go with one

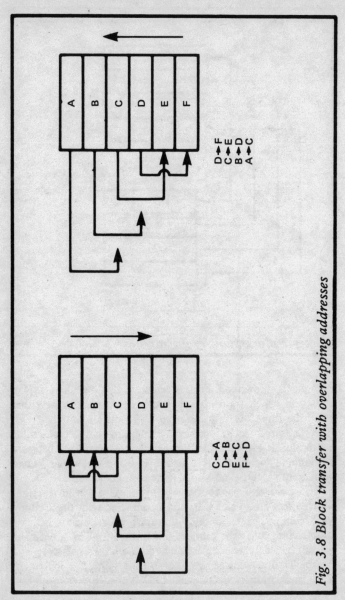

Fig. 3.8 Block transfer with overlapping addresses

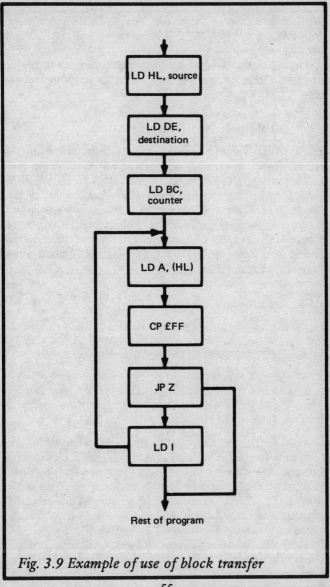

Fig. 3.9 Example of use of block transfer

instruction (compare increment repeat (CPIR) and compare decrement repeat (CPDR)). If a match is found, HL indicates the address.

The block transfer and search instructions are a somewhat advanced technique, but are very useful for handling files and text.

3.4.7 Bit Manipulation

The Z-80 has a comprehensive range of instructions to allow individual bits in registers and store locations to be set, reset and tested. These instructions are particularly useful in control and data handling applications. Register indirect (using HL) and indexed addressing is used for accessing store locations. Bit tests set or reset the zero flag in the F register (Z flag set if tested bit is zero). An example of a bit manipulation instruction is CB 5E which tests bit 3 in the store location whose address is held in register pair HL.

3.4.8 Input/Output

The basis of input/output instructions were described in section 1.5. In a Z-80 based microcomputer, up to 256 I/O ports can be addressed. An I/O instruction has to define:

  i. The port address (8 bits)
 ii. The direction (input or output)
iii. The store location or register which is the source (or destination) of the data.

The Z-80 uses direct addressing and register indirect addressing to specify the port number. D3 05, for example is "output one word to port 5 from register A" (using direct addressing). All indirect addressing is done with register C holding the address. An example of an indirect addressed I/O instruction is ED 60 which is "Input one word from the port whose address is held in register C to register H".

There are also a useful range of block transfer I/O instructions which transfer large chunks of data between sequential store locations and an I/O port. These operate in a similar manner to the block transfer instructions described previously in section 3.4.6.

Register pair HL contains the store address
Register B contains the byte counter
Register C contains the port address

The block transfer instructions are particularly useful for inputting data from (say) a tape recorder or sending data to a printer.

We will return to I/O instructions again in Chapter 6 where I/O support devices are described and section 6.4 where the operation of interrupts is discussed.

3.4.9 Control Instructions

There are six Z-80 control instructions. Four of these are concerned with the operations of interrupts (described further in section 6.4). The remaining two are "Halt" and the dummy "No operation".

3.4.10 General Observations

We have described the Z-80 instructions in very general terms. In Chapter 4 the full instructions set is given in a formal manner.

3.5 SYMBOLIC REPRESENTATION

It is very laborious to describe instructions in a descriptive manner such as "Fetch to register A the contents of the store location whose address is held in register pair HL". A simple, logical symbolism is used to represent instructions in the Z-80 (and other) microprocessors. Typical instructions are represented as.

$$A \leftarrow A + 1$$
$$A \leftarrow A + (HL)$$

Let us see what these symbols mean, and how they

represent an instruction.

Registers are represented by their letters (A, B, C, etc.). Numbers are simply represented by their hex equivalent; 19, C5 for example. The arrow ← shows the data movement, so:

> A ← B means move the contents of register B to register A
>
> C ← 37 means load register C with the hex number 37 (immediate addressing)

Arithmetic operations are represented by these symbols:

+	addition
−	subtraction
∧	and
∨	or
⊕	exclusive or

We can thus write:

> A ← A + 1 Add 1 to the contents of register A
>
> A ← A + B Add the contents of register A and B, result to register A

The contents of store locations are represented by brackets ( ). We therefore interpret (0C50) to mean the contents of store location 0C50. Care should be taken, since FFE1 means a 16 bit humber as in:

> HL ← FFE1 means load register pair HL with hex number FFE1 (immediate addressing)

(FFE1)means the contents of store location FFE1 as in:

> (FFE1) ← B which is store the contents of register B in store location FFE1.

Register indirect and indexed addressing are also represented by ( ) since they refer to store locations. For example:

> B ← (HL) is bring contents of the store location whose address is held in register pair HL to register B (register indirect addressing)

$A \leftarrow A + (IX + 3)$ Add the contents of register A to the contents of the store location whose address is given by adding 3 to the contents of the index register, the result to go to register A.

The last example shows the simplicity of the symbolism!

Even jump instructions can be represented. A simple jump is:

$PC \leftarrow 1DAF$ Jump to location 1DAF (PC stands for program counter)

A subroutine call to a subroutine at F6000 is represented by the three symbols:

$(SP - 1) \leftarrow PC_H$, $(SP - 2) \leftarrow PC_L$; $PC \leftarrow F6000$

SP refers to the stack pointer, PC_H is the high byte of the program counter, PC_L is the low byte of the program counter.

The symbolism cannot be used to represent shift instruction and control instructions.

3.6 CONCLUSION

In this chapter we have described the Z-80 instructions and addressing modes in a descriptive manner. In chapter 4 the complete instruction set is given formally in a manner suitable for reference by a programmer.

Chapter Four

THE Z-80 INSTRUCTION SET

4.1 INTRODUCTION

In Chapter 3 the Z-80 instruction set was described in narrative fashion. In this chapter the full instruction set is given in a formal fashion. The most convenient way to do this is in tabular form. Most instructions involve data from some source (a register, a port or a store location) and the result goes to a destination. The instructions are represented in the form of tables with the data source across the top and the destination down the side. The instruction (in Hex code) can then be read off like a car mileage chart. On Table 4.1, for example, the code to move data from register E to register B is 43.

In the tables, "n" refers to a single byte hex number (i.e. two hex digits) "n" is used for immediate data and port addressing. "nn" refers to a double byte hex number (i.e. four hex digits) "nn" is used for extended addressing and 16 bit immediate data. "d" is used for the (single byte) offset in indexed instructions (representing a signed twos complement number, remember) "e" is used for the displacement in relative addressing.

Where two byte numbers "nn" are used, it should be remembered that the low byte comes first. C3 50 0C is a jump instruction to 0C 50, for example.

It should also be remembered that brackets ( ) refer to store locations, so (BC) indicates register indirect addressing, with register pair BC holding the store location.

Assembler mnemonics are also given with the tables, although Z-80 assembly language is not described until chapter 5. The tables are intended for reference purposes, and would not be complete without the assembler mnemonics.

The Z-80 is a development of the Intel 8080 microprocessor, and all 8080 instructions are available on the Z-80. These instructions have a small identifier in the top left hand corner of the instruction box in the table.

4.2 LOAD INSTRUCTIONS

4.2.1 8 bit Loads

The full set of 8 bit load instructions is shown on Table 4.1.
As explained previously, the source of the data is given across
the top, and the destination down the side. The code for
$D \leftarrow H$, for example, is 54, and the code for $A \leftarrow 15$ is 3E 15.

All load mnemonics have the form:

LD Destination, Source

for example, LD A,(HL) which has the code 7E.

Note that the instructions to load immediate data into an
indexed address occupies four locations (DD 36 d n and FD 36
d n).

4.2.2 16 bit Loads

The Z-80 can also move 16 bit (2 byte) data between register
pairs and two successive store locations. These 16 bit load
instructions are given on Table 4.2. This is driven in a similar
manner to Table 4.1.

SP refers to the stack pointer. The use of the stack was
explained earlier in section 2.2.4. The PUSH instructions put
data onto the stack, and the POP instruction retrieves data
from the stack. When register pairs are pushed onto the stack,
the order is as below:

First (High)	Second (Low)
A	F
B	C
D	E
H	L

When a push instruction is obeyed, the sequence of events
is.

Table 4.1 8 Bit Load Group
Instruction Mnemonics are all LD destination, source

		IMPLIED		REGISTER				
		I	R	A	B	C	D	E
REGISTER	A	ED 57	ED 5F	7F	78	79	7A	7B
	B			47	40	41	42	43
	C			4F	48	49	4A	4B
	D			57	50	51	52	53
	E			5F	58	59	5A	5B
	H			67	60	61	62	63
	L			6F	68	69	6A	6B
REG. INDIRECT	(HL)			77	70	71	72	73
	(BC)			02				
	(DE)			12				
INDEXED	(IX+d)			DD 77 d	DD 70 d	DD 71 d	DD 72 d	DD 73 d
	(IY+d)			FD 77 d	FD 70 d	FD 71 d	FD 72 d	FD 73 d
EXT. ADD.	(nn)			32 n n				
IMPLIED	I			ED 47				
	R			ED 4F				

DESTINATION

Note: Reg. Indirect, Indexed & Ext. Addressing access the store

H	L	REG. INDIRECT			INDEXED		EXT. ADDR.	IMMED.
		(HL)	(BC)	(DE)	(IX+d)	(IY+d)	(nn)	n
7C	7D	7E	0A	1A	DD 7E d	FD 7E d	3A n n	3E n
44	45	46			DD 46 d	FD 46 d		06 n
4C	4D	4E			DD 4E d	FD 4E d		0E n
54	55	56			DD 56 d	FD 56 d		16 n
5C	5D	5E			DD 5E d	FD 5E d		1E n
64	65	66			DD 66 d	FD 66 d		26 n
6C	6D	6E			DD 6E d	FD 6E d		2E n
74	75							36 n
DD 74 d	DD 75 d							DD 36 d n
FD 74 d	FD 75 d							FD 36 d n

Table 4.2 16 Bit Load Group (includes PUSH & POP)

Instruction Mnemonics are: LD destination, source;
POP register pair; PUSH register pair

		SOURCE								IMM. EXT.	EXT. ADDR.	REG. INDIR.
		REGISTER										
		AF	BC	DE	HL	SP	IX	IY	nn	(nn)	(SP)
DESTINATION / REGISTER	AF										F1
	BC								01 n n	ED 4B n n	C1
	DE								11 n n	ED 5B n n	D1
	HL								21 n n	2A n n	E1
	SP				F9		DD F9	FD F9	31 n n	ED 7B n n	
	IX								DD 21 n n	DD 2A n n	DD E1
	IY								FD 21 n n	FD 2A n n	FD E1
EXT. ADDR.	(nn)		ED 43 n n	ED 53 n n	22 n n	ED 73 n n	DD 22 n n	FD 22 n n			
REG. INDIR.	(SP)	F5	C5	D5	E5		DD E5	FD E5			←PUSH

↑
POP

Note: Push subtracts 2 from SP; Pop adds 2 to SP; LDs to & from
store use 2 locations for data; Ext. and Reg. Indir. access the store

> Decrement SP
> Store High byte in (SP)
> Decrement SP
> Store Low byte in (SP)

When a pop instruction is obeyed, the sequence is:

> Retrieve Low Byte from (SP)
> Increment SP
> Retrieve High Byte from (SP)
> Increment SP

16 bit loads have the same assembler mnemonic as the 8 bit
loads, LD Destination, Source. The push instruction
mnemonics have the form Push Register Pair (e.g. PUSH AF).

64

The Pop instructions mnemonics have the form POP Register Pair (e.g. POP HL).

4.2.3 Exchanges

The Z-80 has two register sets as explained in section 2.2. The exchange instructions switch between these with two instructions. The first interchanges AF and AF'. The second interchanges BC, BC'; DE, DE'; HL, HL'. Both are one byte instructions.

There are four other exchange instructions which interchange data between register pairs, or a register pair and the stack. The contents of HL and DE can be interchanged, and contents of HL, IX, IY interchanged with the bottom two bytes of the stack (leaving the stack pointer unchanged).

Table 4.3 shows the six exchange instructions.

Table 4.3   Exchanges
Instruction Mnemonics EX, EXX

		IMPLIED ADDRESSING				
		AF'	BC', DE' & HL'	HL	IX	IY
IMPLIED	AF	08				
	BC, DE & HL		D9 EXX Mnemonic			
	DE			EB		
Reg. Indir.	(SP)			E3	DD E3	FD E3

↑
Exchanges data with stack

65

4.3 ARITHMETIC AND LOGIC INSTRUCTIONS

4.3.1 8 Bit Instructions

The Z-80 arithmetic and logic instructions were described informally in section 3.4.3. The full range is shown on Table 4.4. Note that with the exception of CP, INC and DEC instructions the result always goes to Register A. Data can only be obtained from store locations with register indirect (HL as pointer) or indexed addressing.

Table 4.4 8 Bit Arithmetic & Logic Group

Mnemonic		REGISTER ADDRESSING (SOURCE)						REG. INDIR.	INDEXED		Immed.
	A	B	C	D	E	H	L	(HL)	(IX+d)	(IY+d)	n
ADD	87	80	81	82	83	84	85	86	DD 86 d	FD 86 d	C6 n
ADD w CARRY ADC	8F	88	89	8A	8B	8C	8D	8E	DD 8E d	FD 8E d	CE n
SUBTRACT SUB	97	90	91	92	93	94	95	96	DD 96 d	FD 96 d	D6 n
SUB w CARRY SBC	9F	98	99	9A	9B	9C	9D	9E	DD 9E d	FD 9E d	DE n
AND	A7	A0	A1	A2	A3	A4	A5	A6	DD A6 d	FD A6 d	E6 n
XOR	AF	A8	A9	AA	AB	AC	AD	AE	DD AE d	FD AE d	EE n
OR	B7	B0	B1	B2	B3	B4	B5	B6	DD B6 d	FD B6 d	F6 n
COMPARE CP	BF	B8	B9	BA	BB	BC	BD	BE	DD BE d	FD BE d	FE n
INCREMENT INC	3C	04	0C	14	1C	24	2C	34	DD 34 d	FD 34 d	
DECREMENT DEC	3D	05	0D	15	1D	25	2D	35	DD 35 d	FD 35 d	

DESTINATION: to Reg. A (ADD to COMPARE); Flags; SOURCE (INC, DEC)

Note: Compare only effects flags

4.3.2   General Purpose Operations on AF

There are five instructions shown on Table 4.5 which operate on the accumulator (register A) and the flag register. Each of these require a little explanation.

Table 4.5   General Purpose AF Group

Decimal Adjust Acc, 'DAA'	27
Complement Acc, 'CPL'	2F
Negate Acc, 'NEG' (2's complement)	ED 44
Complement Carry Flag, 'CCF'	3F
Set Carry Flag, 'SCF'	37

4.3.2.1   *Decimal Adjust Accumulator (DAA)*

It is often convenient to represent numbers in Binary Coded Decimal (BCD). This represents each decade by four bits, e.g. decimal 79 would be represented by 0111 1001. Four bits can represent $0 - 15$, so binary codes 1010 to 1111 are not used in BCD, and one byte can only represent 0 to 99 decimal.

If the arithmetic operations in Table 4.4 are used with BCD coded data the wrong answer will result. If, for example, register A contains decimal 47 in BCD (0100 0111), register B contains decimal 26 in BCD (0010 0110) addition will give:

A	0100	0111
B	0010	0110
Result	0110	1101

which is Hex 6D and is not decimal 73 in either BCD or binary!

The decimal adjust instruction corrects the result of a BCD addition or subtraction instruction to give a BCD result. In the example above a DAA instruction on 6D would give the correct BCD result 73. The DAA does *NOT* convert a Hex or binary number to its BCD equivalent.

The DAA corrects the result of a subtraction and addition in a different way, and uses the N flag to determine if the last instruction was an add or subtract. It is therefore very important to use the DAA instruction immediately after the add or subtract instruction which it is to correct.

The DAA instruction itself sets the flags according to the BCD result obtained after the adjustment. For example, if A contained BCD 87 and B contained BCD 26, adding A and B would give Hex AD. A DAA would then give BCD 13 with the carry flag set (decimal 87 + decimal 26 = decimal 113).

4.3.2.2 Complement Accumulator (CPL)
The complement accumulator instruction simply replaces '1's by '0's and vice versa in the accumulator. For example:

  1 0 1 1 0 1 1 1 (B7 hex)   0 1 0 1 0 0 0 1 (51 hex)

becomes

  0 1 0 0 1 0 0 0 (48 hex)   1 0 1 0 1 1 1 0 (AE hex)

CPL is a useful single byte instruction.

4.3.2.3 Negate Accumulator (NEG)
The negate instruction replaces the data in the accumulator by the twos complement number of opposite sign. +23, for example becomes −23.

For example:

> 04 Hex becomes FC Hex (−4)
> E7 Hex (−19 Hex) becomes 19 Hex

4.3.2.4 Complement Carry Flag (CCF), Set Carry Flag (SCF)
These instructions simply allow the state of the carry flag to be changed (CCF) or forced to a '1' (SCF). All other flags remain unchanged.

4.3.3 16 Bit Arithmetic

Table 4.6 shows the range of 16 bit arithmetic instructions available on the Z-80. These operate solely on the register pairs, stack pointer and index register contents. It is not possible to perform (directly) arithmetic operations on 16 bit data in two successive store locations. All register pairs can be incremented and decremented.

Table 4.6 16 Bit Arithmetic Group

DESTINATION		SOURCE: BC	DE	HL	SP	IX	IY
'ADD'	HL	09	19	29	39		
'ADD'	IX	DD 09	DD 19		DD 39	DD 29	
'ADD'	IY	FD 09	FD 19		FD 39		FD 29
Add with Carry and Set Flags 'ADC'	HL	ED 4A	ED 5A	ED 6A	ED 7A		
Sub with Carry and Set Flags 'SBC'	HL	ED 42	ED 52	ED 62	ED 72		
INCREMENT 'INC'		03	13	23	33	DD 23	FD 23
DECREMENT 'DEC'		0B	1B	2B	3B	DD 2B	FD 2B

4.4 JUMP CALL AND RETURN GROUP

The principles of jumps and subroutine calls were outlined in section 3.4.4. The full range is given in Table 4.7. There are 9 conditions available based on the states of the varous flags, although not all conditions are available with every addressing mode.

Table 4.7 Jumps & Subroutine Call & Return

CONDITION

'Mnemonic'			UN-COND.	'C' CARRY	'NC' NON CARRY	'Z' ZERO	'NZ' NON ZERO	'PE' PARITY EVEN	'PO' PARITY ODD	'M' SIGN NEG	'P' SIGN POS	REG B≠0
Jump 'JP'	Immed. Ext.	nn	C3 n n	DA n n	D2 n n	CA n n	C2 n n	EA n n	E2 n n	FA n n	F2 n n	
Jump 'JR'	Relative	PC+e	18 e-2	38 e-2	30 e-2	28 e-2	20 e-2					
Jump 'JP'	Reg. Indir.	(HL)	E9									
Jump 'JP'	Reg. Indir.	(IX)	DD E9									
Jump 'JP'	Reg. Indir.	(IY)	FD E9									
'CALL'	Immed. Ext.	nn	CD n n	DC n n	D4 n n	CC n n	C4 n n	EC n n	E4 n n	FC n n	F4 n n	
Decrement B, Jump if Non Zero "DJNZ"	Relative	PC+e										10 e-2
Return 'RET'	Reg. Indir.	(SP) (SP+1)	C9	D8	D0	C8	C0	E8	E0	F8	F0	
Return from Int 'RETI'	Reg. Indir.	(SP) (SP+1)	ED 4D									
Return from Non Maskable Int 'RETN'	Reg. Indir.	(SP) (SP+1)	ED 45									

Note – Certain Flags have more than one purpose.

Relative addressing can cause some confusion. The offset is calculated from two locations further on from the current location. Twos complement notation is used allowing jumps both forward and backward.

A particularly useful conditional relative jump is the "dec B, jump non zero" (DJNZ) which allows B to be used as a counter when a block of instructions is to be performed a specific number of times. This is called a loop, and is summarised on Fig. 4.1.

Subroutine calls are available with 9 conditions, but are only available with extended addressing. Returns from sub-

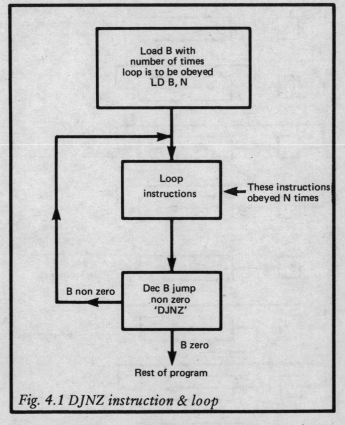

Fig. 4.1 DJNZ instruction & loop

routines are again available with 9 conditions (the return address is, of course, obtained from the stack pointer).

The two remaining return instructions are concerned with interrupts, a topic discussed further in section 6.4.

4.5 SHIFTS AND ROTATES

There are 7 types of shift and rotate instructions summarised on Fig. 4.2.

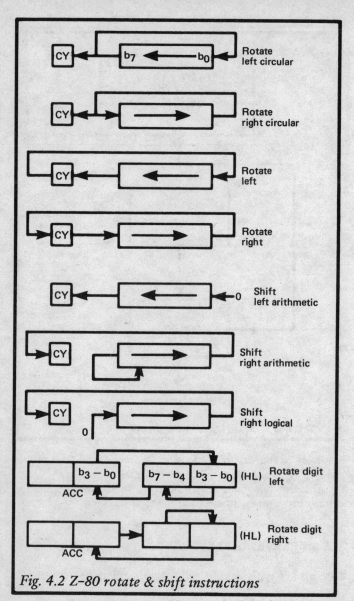

Fig. 4.2 Z–80 rotate & shift instructions

'0' = zero
CY = carry flag
(HL) = store location whose
address is held in HL
ACC = register A (i.e. Accumulator)

Fig. 4.2 (b)

	A
RLCA	07
RRCA	0F
RLA	17
RRA	1F

Table 4.8 Rotate & Shifts Group

SOURCE & DESTINATION

TYPE OF ROTATE or SHIFT	A	B	C	D	E	H	L	(HL)	(IX+d)	(IY+d)
'RLC'	CB 07	CB 00	CB 01	CB 02	CB 03	CB 04	CB 05	CB 06	DD CB d 06	FD CB d 06
'RRC'	CB 0F	CB 08	CB 09	CB 0A	CB 0B	CB 0C	CB 0D	CB 0E	DD CB d 0E	FD CB d 0E
'RL'	CB 17	CB 10	CB 11	CB 12	CB 13	CB 14	CB 15	CB 16	DD CB d 16	FD CB d 16
'RR'	CB 1F	CB 18	CB 19	CB 1A	CB 1B	CB 1C	CB 1D	CB 1E	DD CB d 1E	FD CB d 1E
'SLA'	CB 27	CB 20	CB 21	CB 22	CB 23	CB 24	CB 25	CB 26	DD CB d 26	FD CB d 26
'SRA'	CB 2F	CB 28	CB 29	CB 2A	CB 2B	CB 2C	CB 2D	CB 2E	DD CB d 2E	FD CB d 2E
'SRL'	CB 3F	CB 38	CB 39	CB 3A	CB 3B	CB 3C	CB 3D	CB 3E	DD CB d 3E	FD CB d 3E
'RLD'								ED 6F		
'RRD'								ED 67		

Mnemonic
See Fig. 4.2 for operation

73

These operate as described in section 3.4.5 and are relatively straightforward.

The rotate digit left (RLD) and rotate digit right (RRD) are intended for use with BCD arithmetic and shift four bits between the bottom half of the accumulator and a store location obtained by register indirect addressing with HL containing the address.

Four instructions are duplicated (RLCA, RRCA, RLA, RRA) to include original Intel 8080 instructions.

Table 4.9   Block Transfer Group

None available on 8080
Reg HL points to source
Reg DE points to destination
Reg BC is byte counter

DESTINATION	SOURCE	REG. INDIR. (HL)
REG. INDIR. (DE)	ED A0	'LDI' – Load (DE) ← (HL) Inc HL & DE, Dec BC
	ED B0	'LDIR' – Load (DE) ← (HL) Inc HL & DE, Dec BC, Repeat until BC=0
	ED A8	'LDD' – Load (DE) ← (HL) Dec HL & DE, Dec BC
	ED B8	'LDDR' – Load (DE) ← (HL) Dec HL & DE, Dec BC, Repeat until BC=0

74

4.6 BLOCK TRANSFERS AND SEARCHES

Table 4.9 shows the powerful block transfer instructions. As explained in section 3.4.6, HL is used to hold the source address, DE holds the data address, and BC is a byte counter.

Table 4.10 shows the block search instructions.

Table 4.10   Block Search Group

Search
Location

REG. INDIR. (HL)	
ED A1	'CPI' Inc HL, Dec BC
ED B1	'CPIR', Inc HL, Dec BC repeat until BC=0 or find match
ED A9	'CPD' Dec HL & BC
ED B9	'CPDR' Dec HL & BC Repeat until BC=0 or find match

None available on 8080

HL points to location in memory to be compared
    with accumulator contents
BC is byte counter

4.7 BIT MANIPULATION

The range of bit manipulation instructions are shown on Table 4.11. These allow any bit to be set, reset or tested in any register or (using indirect or indexed addressing) any store location. The test instructions set the Zero Flag if the tested bit is zero.

4.8 INPUT AND OUTPUT GROUP

An input instruction needs to specify the port address and the destination for the data. The Z-80 input instructions, shown on Table 4.12, all have registers as the destination, and the port address specified either by immediate addressing or register indirect with register C holding the port address. A single byte is used as a port address, so 256 ports can be addressed. The contents of register A appear on the top 8 bits of the address bus giving 64K of port addressing for more ambitious users!

There are also a useful range of block input instructions. These operate in a similar manner to the block transfer instructions, and are used to input a block of data from a port to sequential store locations. Register pair HL holds the store address, register B is used as a counter and register C holds the port address.

The output instructions, shown on Table 4.13, transfer data from registers to a specified port address. As above, immediate and indirect addressing is used.

There is again a range of block output instructions which output a block of data from sequential store locations to a specified port. Register pair HL holds the store address, register B is used as a counter and register C holds the port address.

Input/Output is a somewhat involved topic that is dealt with further in chapter 6 where actual I/O devices are described along with the operation of interrupts.

Table 4.11 Bit Manipulation Group

			REGISTER ADDRESSING						REG. INDIR.	INDEXED	
	Bit	A	B	C	D	E	H	L	(HL)	(IX+d)	(IY+d)
TEST 'BIT'	0	CB 47	CB 40	CB 41	CB 42	CB 43	CB 44	CB 45	CB 46	DD CB d 46	FD CB d 46
	1	CB 4F	CB 48	CB 49	CB 4A	CB 4B	CB 4C	CB 4D	CB 4E	DD CB d 4E	FD CB d 4E
	2	CB 57	CB 50	CB 51	CB 52	CB 53	CB 54	CB 55	CB 56	DD CB d 56	FD CB d 56
	3	CB 5F	CB 58	CB 59	CB 5A	CB 5B	CB 5C	CB 5D	CB 5E	DD CB d 5E	FD CB d 5E

Cont...

77

Cont . . .

Operation	Bit	A	B	C	D	E	H	L	(HL)	(IX+d)	(IY+d)
TEST 'BIT'	4	CB 67	CB 60	CB 61	CB 62	CB 63	CB 64	CB 65	CB 66	DD CB d 66	FD CB d 66
	5	CB 6F	CB 68	CB 69	CB 6A	CB 6B	CB 6C	CB 6D	CB 6E	DD CB d 6E	FD CB d 6E
	6	CB 77	CB 70	CB 71	CB 72	CB 73	CB 74	CB 75	CB 76	DD CB d 76	FD CB d 76
	7	CB 7F	CB 78	CB 79	CB 7A	CB 7B	CB 7C	CB 7D	CB 7E	DD CB d 7E	FD CB d 7E
RESET BIT 'RES'	0	CB 87	CB 80	CB 81	CB 82	CB 83	CB 84	CB 85	CB 86	DD CB d 86	FD CB d 86
	1	CB 8F	CB 88	CB 89	CB 8A	CB 8B	CB 8C	CB 8D	CB 8E	DD CB d 8E	FD CB d 8E
	2	CB 97	CB 90	CB 91	CB 92	CB 93	CB 94	CB 95	CB 96	DD CB d 96	FD CB d 96

Operation	Bit									
RESET BIT 'RES'	3	CB 9F	CB 98	CB 99	CB 9A	CB 9B	CB 9C	CB 9D	CB 9E	DD CB d 9E / FD CB d 9E
	4	CB A7	CB A0	CB A1	CB A2	CB A3	CB A4	CB A5	CB A6	DD CB d A6 / FD CB d A6
	5	CB AF	CB A8	CB A9	CB AA	CB AB	CB AC	CB AD	CB AE	DD CB d AE / FD CB d AE
	6	CB B7	CB B0	CB B1	CB B2	CB B3	CB B4	CB B5	CB B6	DD CB d B6 / FD CB d B6
	7	CB BF	CB B8	CB B9	CB BA	CB BB	CB BC	CB BD	CB BE	DD CB d BE / FD CB d BE
SET BIT 'SET'	0	CB C7	CB C0	CB C1	CB C2	CB C3	CB C4	CB C5	CB C6	DD CB d C6 / FD CB d C6
	1	CB CF	CB C8	CB C9	CB CA	CB CB	CB CC	CB CD	CB CE	DD CB d CE / FD CB d CE

Cont...

2	CB D7	CB D0	CB D1	CB D2	CB D3	CB D4	CB D5	CB D6	DD CB d D6	FD CB d D6
3	CB DF	CB D8	CB D9	CB DA	CB DB	CB DC	CB DD	CB DE	DD CB d DE	FD CB d DE
4	CB E7	CB E0	CB E1	CB E2	CB E3	CB E4	CB E5	CB E6	DD CB d E6	FD CB d E6
5	CB EF	CB E8	CB E9	CB EA	CB EB	CB EC	CB ED	CB EE	DD CB d EE	FD CB d EE
6	CB F7	CB F0	CB F1	CB F2	CB F3	CB F4	CB F5	CB F6	DD CB d F6	FD CB d F6
7	CB FF	CB F8	CB F9	CB FA	CB FB	CB FC	CB FD	CB FE	DD CB d FE	FD CB d FE

SET BIT 'SET'

Instruction Mnemonic have form BIT n, source
RES n, source
SET n, source

None available on 8080

80

Table 4.12　Input Group

			PORT ADDRESS	
			IMMED	REG. INDIR.
			n	(C)
INPUT DESTINATION	INPUT 'IN' REG ADDRESSING	A	DB n	ED 78
		B		ED 40
		C		ED 48
		D		ED 50
		E		ED 58
		H		ED 60
		L		ED 68
	'INI' – INPUT & Inc HL. Dec B	(HL) REG. INDIR.		ED A2	BLOCK INPUT COMMANDS
	'INIR' – INP, inc HL, Dec B, Repeat if B $\neq$ 0			ED B2
	'IND' – INPUT & Dec. HL, Dec B			ED AA
	'INDR' – INPUT, Dec HL, Dec B, Repeat if B $\neq$ 0			ED BA

Table 4.13 Output Group

SOURCE

			REGISTER							REG. IND.
	Immed.		A	B	C	D	E	H	L	(HL)
	n	(C)	D3 n							
'OUT'	Reg. Ind.	(C)	ED 79	ED 41	ED 49	ED 51	ED 59	ED 61	ED 69	
'OUTI' – OUTPUT Inc. HL, Dec B	Reg. Ind.	(C)								ED A3
'OTIR' – OUTPUT, Inc HL Dec. B, Repeat if B≠0	Reg. Ind.	(C)								ED B3
'OUTD' – OUTPUT Dec HL & B	Reg. Ind.	(C)								ED AB
'OTDR' – OUTPUT, Dec HL & B, Repeat if B≠0	Reg. Ind.	(C)								ED BB

PORT DESTINATION ADDRESS

BLOCK OUTPUT COMMANDS

4.9 RESTARTS

The restart instructions are a special group of subroutine calls. The 8 restart instructions, shown on Table 4.14, call subroutines at hex addresses 0, 8, 10, 18, 20, 28, 30, and 38. Commonly used subroutines can be placed at these addresses and called with single byte instructions.

Table 4.14 Restart Group

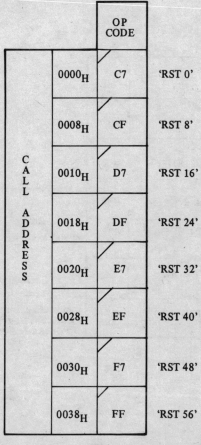

CALL ADDRESS	OP CODE	
0000_H	C7	'RST 0'
0008_H	CF	'RST 8'
0010_H	D7	'RST 16'
0018_H	DF	'RST 24'
0020_H	E7	'RST 32'
0028_H	EF	'RST 40'
0030_H	F7	'RST 48'
0038_H	FF	'RST 56'

4.10   CONTROL INSTRUCTIONS

The 6 Z-80 control instructions are shown on Table 4.15. The no-operation instruction is simply skipped. This is actually more useful than might be first thought, as it allows gaps (for corrections) to be left in programs. HALT, stops the operation of the processor until an interrupt is received or the reset signal (pin 26) is given. The remaining control instructions are concerned with interrupts and are described in section 6.4.

Table 4.15   CPU Control Group

Instruction	Code	Description
'NOP'	00	
'HALT'	76	
DISABLE INT '(DI)'	F3	
ENABLE INT '(EI)'	FB	
SET INT MODE 0 'IM0'	ED 46	8080A Mode
SET INT MODE 1 'IM1'	ED 56	Call to Location 0038$_H$
SET INT MODE 2 'IM2'	ED 5E	Indirect Call using Register I and 8 bits from Interrupting Device as a Pointer.

4.11   GENERAL OBSERVATIONS

We have now covered all the Z-80 instructions. It cannot be over-emphasised that it is not practical (or even desirable) to learn them by heart. It is best for the beginner to start by writing very simple programs using just a small selection from the Z-80 repertoire to gain experience. Do not start by writing a 32K adventure program!

In the following chapter we will describe the Z-80 Assembler Language which simplifies machine code programming.

Chapter Five

ASSEMBLY LANGUAGE PROGRAMMING

5.1 INTRODUCTION

Programming in the actual hex machine code is tedious and error prone. It is not difficult to see why working in machine code causes problems. Consider the simple program below:

> 3A 50 0C A1 FE 01 C2 00 1D

To find out what this does we must determine where each instruction starts and finishes. By laborious reference to chapter 4 we get:

3A 50 0C	Load A from location 0C50
A1	And with the contents of register C
FE 01	Compare with '01'
C2 00 1D	Jump if zero flag is not set to instruction at 1D00

Understanding a bald Hex program is not easy, and is doubly difficult with a program written by someone else.

Another problem occurs when a program requires to be modified due either to a fault or to changed requirements. Unlike BASIC, the simple insertion of one instruction to a machine code program will affect the addresses of all subsequent instructions, with unfortunate repercussions on the destination of jump instructions. This problem can be alleviated to some extent by leaving gaps at strategic places in a program, but the requirement to insert an instruction will always make a programmer wince.

Machine code programs can be made comprehensible and easy to modify if the programmer uses a programming aid called an Assembler, which allows machine code programs initially to be written in a form closer to a high level language such as BASIC.

In assembly language, programs are written using mnemonics for each and every machine code instruction.

Examples of these mnemonics are:

    LD   Load, i.e. data movement
    CALL Subroutine Call
    JP   Jump
    ADD   Arithmetic Additions

The program written in mnemonics is called the source program. The programmer loads a special program called an Assembler into his computer, followed by his source program. The assembler converts the source program mnemonics into their machine code equivalent (not a particularly difficult operation, actually, as there is a one to one relationship between the mnemonics and their Hex coding). The resultant machine code program is called the object program, and can usually be saved on cassette, disc or paper tape, or transferred direct to the computer store.

Writing a program in assembly language is therefore very similar to writing a program in BASIC, except that one BASIC instruction will be the equivalent of many machine code instructions, whereas one instruction in the source program will represent one, and only one, machine code instruction.

Assembly language programming is much easier than straight machine code. The use of mnemonics makes the program easier to understand, and the assembler allows instructions to be added or deleted during debugging, with the computer adjusting all the jump instructions. Anyone seriously contemplating machine code programming should therefore aim to obtain an assembler.

There are many different assemblers for the Z-80 with slight differences in syntax, as there are many slightly different versions of BASIC. This chapter is therefore a non formal introduction to the principles of assembly language programming. With the background provided in this chapter, the reader should have little difficulty in following the formal presentation of any assembler language instruction manual.

5.2 THE SOURCE PROGRAM

5.2.1 Introduction

There are slight differences between manufacturers assemblers as there are between different BASICs, but in general, one source program instruction has the form:

Line Number   Label   Instruction Mnemonic,   Comments

For example, we could have:

70 LOOP ADD HL,DE;ADD MULTICAND TO RESULT

The line number is 70
The label identifying the location holding the instruction is LOOP.
Labels are optional.
The instruction menmonic is ADD HL,DE (add the contents of register pairs HL and DE, result to HL)

The comments always follow after a semicolon and are optional. Although they are not used by the assembler as such, good comments are essential to the understanding of the program at a later date.

It is most important to remember that one source code instruction represents one machine code instruction. The above example would be converted to the machine code instruction 19 (see Table 4.6).

We will now consider each item in a source program instruction in more detail.

5.2.2 Line Numbers

Each source program instruction starts with a line number. Users of BASIC will be familiar with the idea of line numbers, and will be pleased to know that line numbers in assembly language programming are used to identify the order of the instructions in the same way as BASIC.

If we were to type:

```
10 START  LD B, 16; INITIALISE REGISTER B
20        LD HL, 0; CLEAR REGISTER PAIR HL
etc.
```

During debugging, suppose we found that we should also have cleared register A. We would then reload the source program from tape (or disc) and add:

```
15        LD A, 0; CLEAR REGISTER A
```

The source program would now be:

```
10 START  LD B, 16; INITIALISE REGISTER B
15        LD A, 0; CLEAR REGISTER A
20        LD HL, 0; CLEAR REGISTER PAIR HL
```

with line number 15 having been inserted between line numbers 10 and 20. (As an aside LD A,0 gives the machine code instruction 3E 00; two bytes. A shorter instruction with the same result is XOR A, exclusive OR of A with itself, which gives the machine code instruction AF, just one byte). A new object program could now be produced.

The use of line numbers allows instructions to be added, deleted and edited in a similar manner to BASIC. Line numbers are not, however, used in jump instructions (e.g. the BASIC instruction GOTO 120). Labels described in the next section, are used for this purpose.

5.2.3 Labels

Labels are used to identify a store location for use by other instructions (usually jumps and subroutine calls, although any instruction can use a label). We could for example have:

```
JP    RESET
CALL  KBD
LD A, DATA
```

where RESET, KBD, DATA are labels defined elsewhere in the program.

The label can usually be up to 6 letters long, and are chosen to be meaningful to the programmer. There are a few restrictions on labels; usually they must start with a letter and must not contain an instruction mnemonic. Individual assemblers will define allowed formats for labels.

Labels can also be used in an expression to define a store location. For example JP TABLE+7 is a jump instruction to the location seven locations further on from the instruction whose label is TABLE. A special label often used with relative jumps is $ for "this location". For example JRNC Start – $ is a conditional relative jump to Start.

It is not essential (or even desirable) for each and every instruction to be given labels.

5.2.4 Instruction Mnemonic

The instruction mnemonic defines the actual instruction. In chapter 3 we saw that most Z-80 instructions define three things:

  i.   The operation to be performed
  ii. The source (s) for the data to be manipulated
  iii. The destination for the result.

The operation to be performed is defined by a simple easy to remember mnemonic. Examples are:

  LD for load instructions; CALL for subroutine calls;
  ADC for Add with carry; JP for jump; INC for increment.

There are actually only a small number of these mnemonics, as shown on Table 5.1.

Table 5.1   Z-80 MNEMONICS IN ALPHABETICAL ORDER

ADC	Add with Carry
ADD	Add
AND	Logical AND
BIT	Test Bit
CALL	Call Subroutine

CCF	Complement Carry Flag
CP	Compare
CPD	
CPDR	
CPI	Block Search
CPIR	
CPL	Complement Acc
DAA	Decimal Adjust
DEC	Decrement
DI	Disable Interrupts
DJNZ	Dec B Jump Non Zero
EI	Enable Interrupts
EX	Exchange
HALT	HALT
IM	Set Interrupt Mode
IN	Input from port
INC	Increment
IND	
INDR	
INI	Block Input
INIR	
JP	Jump
JR	Jump Relative
LD	Load (Data Movement)
LDD	
LDDR	
LDI	Block Load
LDIR	
NEG	Negate Acc
NOP	No operation
OR	Logical OR
OTDR	
OTIR	Block Output
OUT	Output to port
OUTD	
OUTI	Block Output
POP	Data from stack
PUSH	Data to stack
RES	Reset Bit

RET	Return from subroutine
RETI	Return from interrupt
RETN	Return from NMI
RL	Rotate Left
RR	Rotate Right
RST	Restart
SBC	Subtract with carry
SCF	Set Carry Flag
SET	Set Bit
SLA	Shift left arithmetic
SRA	Shift right arithmetic
SRL	Shift right logical
SUB	Subtract
XOR	Exclusive OR

The full list of mnemonics is given in Appendix B.

The source and destination are represented in a similar manner to the symbolism outlined in section 3.5. Registers and register pairs are represented by their letters; A, B, HL etc. Store locations are represented by brackets ( ). We thus get:

LD A, D	Load register A with the contents of register D
LD (HL), A	Load the store location whose address is held in register pair HL with the contents of register A (register indirect addressing)
ADD B	Add the contents of register B to the contents of register A (all arithmetic operation results go to register A, so the destination is not specified)
SUB 15	Subtract decimal 15 from register A (Immediate addressing)

All numbers in an assembler source program are assumed to be in decimal. Hex numbers are usually preceeded by a Pound (£) sign.

1972 is thus a decimal number
£1972 is thus a hexadecimal number

Some advanced assemblers also allow representation of numbers in octal (base 8) or binary, but these are rather uncommon.

Labels can also be used with the menmonics to specify store locations as explained in the previous section.

Appendix B gives all the instruction mnemonics used by Z-80 assemblers.

5.2.5 Comments

Comments are usually preceeded by a ; to tell the assembler where the instruction menmonic finishes and the comment starts (cf. the REM in BASIC). Comments, although optional should be used liberally and intelligently. In particular, the comments should say what the instruction is doing, and not be just an expanded version of the mnemonic. For example:

```
120 SETUP LD HL, £0C50; START OF STRING 0C50
130        LD B, 36 ;36 CHARACTERS TO BE SENT
```

means a lot more than a simple

```
120 SETUP LD HL, £0C50 ; LOAD HL WITH £0C50
130        LD B, 36 ; LOAD B WITH 36
```

The only problem with comments is that (like all the source program) they have to be stored in the computer prior to assembly. Extensive comments will cause the source program to occupy considerably more store than the resulting object program. This could be a problem in computers with a small store.

5.3 PSEUDO OP CODES

Appendix B defines all the mnemonics corresponding to the Z-80 machine code instructions. In addition to these, assemblers have several pseudo mnemonics which are directions to the assembler itself rather than Z-80 instructions. These are known as pseudo op codes, and are used to indicate where the object code program is to be placed in memory, load alphanumeric strings (i.e. messages) directly and similar operations.

The first of these pseudo op codes is ORG for Origin, which indicates to the assembler where the object program is to start. For example, with

```
100        ORG £4000 ; PROGRAM STARTS 4000
110 PROG   LD A,£FF;MAKE A MINUS ONE
etc.
```

The ORG instruction tells the assembler that the program is to be loaded from Hex 4000 onwards. The LD A,£FF (3E FF) will go into locations 4000 and 4001, followed by the rest of the program.

Several ORG statements can be used in one program.

The second pseudo op code is EQU, for Equate, which is used to equate a label and a value.

An example of the use of EQU occurs where useful subroutines are provided in the ROM of the computer. Let us assume that there is a keyboard reading subroutine in the ROM at Hex 01AF. We would put somewhere at the start of the source program:

(line number) KBD EQU £01AF

Thereafter, when we wish to call the keyboard subroutine we simply write:

(line number) CALL KBD

which the assembler interprets as CALL £01AF. Note how the use of the label KBD assists the comprehensibility.

DEFS (for define space) is the third pseudo op code, and is used to reserve a number of store locations. For example, with:

```
320        JP KBD
330 SPARE  DEFS £100; 100 PLACES FOR DATA
340        CALL LOOP
```

the assembler will leave Hex 100 locations between the jump instruction and the subroutine call.

DEFM (for define message) allows the user to load ASCII values direct from the keyboard. For example:

```
100         ORG £3000
110 DATA  DEFM "ABCD"
```

will put Hex 41 into location 3000 (i.e. ASCII A)
          Hex 42 into location 3001 (i.e. ASCII B)
          Hex 43 into location 3002 (i.e. ASCII C)
          Hex 44 into location 3003 (i.e. ASCII D)

DEFM is very useful for loading fixed messages.

DEFB (define byte) and DEFW (define word) allow the user to define an 8 bit byte or a 16 bit word respectively.

Superficially these are similar to EQU, but the DEF instructions cause data to be loaded as part of the program, whereas the EQU has no action outside of the assembler.

5.4   ASSEMBLER DIRECTIVES

Directives are instructions to the assembler (in the same way as LIST, RUN, EDIT etc. are directives in BASIC). There are, of course, differences between assemblers on different machines, but most will have the following:

    i. Enter a source program
   ii. List a source program to VDU or printer
  iii. Edit a source program (add, delete or modify lines)
  iv. Search for a specific instruction
   v. Renumber a source program (i.e. put all the line numbers in increments of ten)
  vi. Assemble the source program to produce an object program which can be sent to tape, disc or printer or placed directly in the store if space permits.

These directives are selected by keywords from the keyboard in a similar manner to BASIC.

5.5 USING AN ASSEMBLER

To demonstrate how an assembler is used, we shall write a small subroutine using a Z-80 assembler called ZEAP on a Nascom microcomputer. The subroutine is a simple Bubble Sort which sorts data in successive store locations into numerical order. First let us describe the subroutine operation.

The subroutine is entered with register pair HL containing the first address of the data to be sorted, and register C containing the number of items to be sorted. The data is to be left in the original area of store after the sort has been completed, with the smallest number in the lowest store location.

A bubble sort is the simplest and least efficient method of performing a sort, but is relatively easy to understand. The algorithm for a bubble sort can be expressed:

i. Set Marker = 0
ii. Go through the list comparing adjacent pairs. If a pair is in the wrong order interchange them and set Marker = 1
iii. Repeat step ii. until the end of the list
iv. If, at the end of the list, Marker = 1 go back to step i. If Marker = 0 (indicating no changes have been made) the sort is complete

The algorithm might be a bit indigestible for a first reading, and is given in flowchart form in Fig.5.1.

We must now convert this simply expressed flow chart to a machine code program. The routine is entered with the address of the first item in the list held in register pair HL, and the number of items held in register C. The list is accessed using indexed addressing. The items for comparison are held in registers A and E. Register B is used as a counter to see if all the list has been tested (this allows the useful DJNZ (Dec B jump not zero) instruction to be used. Bit 0 in register H is used as the marker to indicate if an exchange has occurred and another pass through the list is required.

The general flow chart of Fig.5.1 is redrawn in a form suitable for machine code programming on Fig.5.2. This can be converted more or less directly to an assembler source program as follows. The reader should carefully compare this

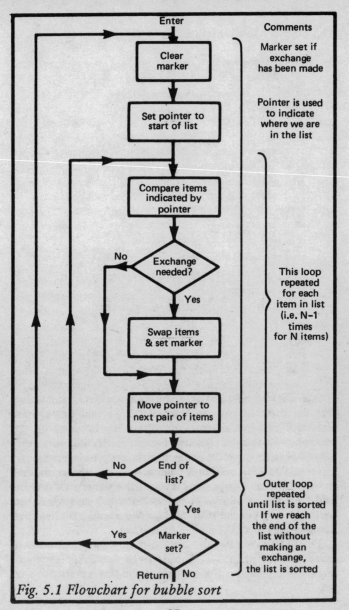

Fig. 5.1 Flowchart for bubble sort

with Fig.5.2 before reading further.

```
0010 ;*** BUBBLE SORT ROUTINE ***
0020 ;ENTER WITH FIRST ITEM ADDRESS IN HL
0030 ;NUMBER OF ITEMS IN C (2 TO 255)
0040 ;EXIT WITH:
0050 ;ITEMS SORTED IN SAME STORE BLOCK
0060 ;HL AND C UNCHANGED
0070 ;REGISTERS A B E IX USED
0080 ;OTHER REGISTERS UNCHANGED
0090 ;
0100 SORT ORG £5000;ADDRESS FOR ROUTINE
0110  LD (FIRST),HL;SAVE ADDRESS TO FREE H
0120 MAIN RES MARK,H;CLEAR EXCHANGE MARKER
0130  LD B,C;SET UP COUNTER FOR TESTS
0140  DEC B;COMPARISONS 1 LESS THAN ITEMS
0150  LD IX,(FIRST);SET IX TO START OF LIST
0160 NEXT LD A,(IX+0);GET FIRST OF PAIR
0170  LD E,(IX+1);GET SECOND OF PAIR
0180  CMP E;COMPARE THEM
0190  JR NC NOEX-$;EXCHANGE NEEDED?
0200  LD (IX+0),E;YES, PUT BACK EXCHANGED
0210  LD (IX+1),A;DITTO
0220  SET MARK,H;MARKER SHOWS EXCHANGE MADE
0230 NOEX INC IX;SET IX FOR NEXT PAIR
0240  DJNZ NEXT-$;JUMP BACK IF NOT END LIST
0250  BIT MARK,H;END REACHED,EXCHANGE MADE?
0260  JR NZ,MAIN-$;GO BACK IF EXCHANGE MADE
0270  LD HL,(FIRST);SORT DONE,RESTORE HL
0280  RET;EXIT FROM SUBROUTINE
0290 ;DEFINITIONS
0300 MARK EQU 0;NAME FOR EXCHANGE MARKER
0310 FIRST DEFS 2;TEMP STORE FIRST ADDRESS
0320 ;
0330 ;
0340 ;
0350 ;
0360 ;
0370 ;
0380 ;
0390 ;
```

The above listing has three errors in it; two grammatical
that the assembler will reject as not being a valid instruction.
The third is a logical error. As written the routine will not
perform a bubble sort correctly under all conditions. "Un-
aware" of these errors let us see how the program operates.

Lines 10 to 90 are simply comments to explain the routine
and the registers is uses. This is essential if the routine is to be
held as part of a subroutine library. Line 100 says where the
routine is to go in the store, and is given a label SORT so that
a main program could simply CALL SORT.

Line 110 saves the list start address in a store location
called FIRST, defined in line 310. The exchange occurred
marker is actually bit 0 in register H and this is cleared at line
120.

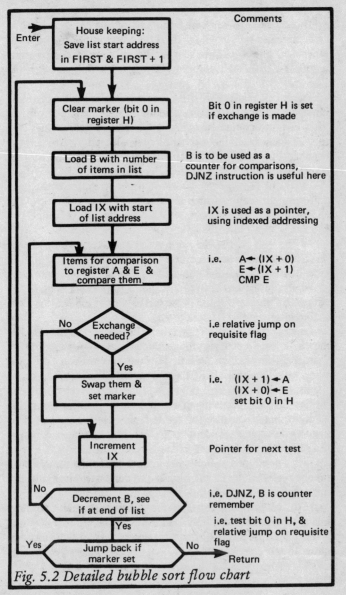

Fig. 5.2 Detailed bubble sort flow chart

99

The counter to see when the end of the list is reached is held in register B to allow the DJNZ instruction to be used. Lines 130 and 140 initialise B. The number of comparisons is one less than the number of items, hence the need for line 140.

The index register IX is used to address the list, and this is initialised at line 150. Lines 160 and 170 bring pairs from the list which are compared at line 180. Line 190 skips lines 200 to 220 inclusive if no exchange is needed. If an exchange is needed, lines 200 and 210 put the data back in the list reversed and line 220 sets the exchange marker.

Line 230 increments the index register ready for the next pair, and the counter in B is decremented at line 240. If the end of the list has not been reached, we jump back to line 160 (the label NEXT) for the next pair.

At the end of the list we look at the exchange marker at line 250. If this is set, line 260 takes us back to line 220 (the label MAIN) for another pass through the list.

When the list has been sorted, line 270 puts HL back to the address at the start of the (now sorted) list so the routine exits with registers C and HL unaltered.

Lines 300 and 310 define labels. Line 300 says that MARK means 0, so we can say, for example, SET MARK, H rather than the less obvious SET 0, H. Line 310 reserves two locations with the labels FIRST (used to hold the start address of the list).

The first step in using an assembler is to load the assembler itself from tape or disc (or call it if you are lucky enough to have an assembler resident in ROM). The source program is then typed in.

It is a good idea to immediately save the source program on tape, to prevent teeth gnashing if the computer crashes or the mains fails during testing.

With the protection of a back up source program, we now ask the assembler to convert the source program to a machine code object program. Not surprisingly, this is known as assembling. In our case we get:

100

```
500B ERROR 30 0160 NEXT    LD   A,(IX+O)

500E ERROR 20 0180         CMP  E
```

This indicates that we have grammatical errors in our program. Different assemblers indicate errors in different ways, but ZEAP uses error codes.

On line 160 an error 30 was given. This indicates a label not found. In fact, IX + 0 has been incorrectly entered with letter O instead of a figure 0. The assembler has looked unsuccessfully for a label letter O. A typical typing error.

One line 180 we have error 20. This indicates that the assembler could not recognize the mnemonic. The correct mnemonic for compare is CP not CMP. A typical pilot error.

With these errors corrected, we ask for another assembly which gives

```
                0010 ;*** BUBBLE SORT ROUTINE ***
                0020 ;ENTER WITH FIRST ITEM ADDRESS IN HL
                0030 ;NUMBER OF ITEMS IN C (2 TO 255)
                0040 ;EXIT WITH:
                0050 ;ITEMS SORTED IN SAME STORE BLOCK
                0060 ;HL AND C UNCHANGED
                0070 ;REGISTERS A B E IX USED
                0080 ;OTHER REGISTERS UNCHANGED
                0090 ;
5000            0100 SORT  ORG  £5000;ADDRESS FOR ROUTINE
5000 222850     0110       LD   (FIRST),HL;SAVE ADDRESS TO FREE H
5003 CB84       0120 MAIN  RES  MARK,H;CLEAR EXCHANGE MARKER
5005 41         0130       LD   B,C;SET UP COUNTER FOR TESTS
5006 05         0140       DEC  B;COMPARISONS 1 LESS THAN ITEMS
5007 DD2A2850   0150       LD   IX,(FIRST);SET IX TO START OF LIST
500B DD7E00     0160 NEXT  LD   A,(IX+0);GET FIRST OF PAIR
500E DD5E01     0170       LD   E,(IX+1);GET SECOND OF PAIR
5011 BB         0180       CP   E;COMPARE THEM
5012 3008       0190       JR   NC NOEX-$;EXCHANGE NEEDED?
5014 DD7300     0200       LD   (IX+0),E;YES, PUT BACK EXCHANGED
5017 DD7701     0210       LD   (IX+1),A;DITTO
501A CBC4       0220       SET  MARK,H;MARKER SHOWS EXCHANGE MADE
501C DD23       0230 NOEX  INC  IX;SET IX FOR NEXT PAIR
501E 10EB       0240       DJNZ NEXT-$;JUMP BACK IF NOT END LIST
5020 CB44       0250       BIT  MARK,H;END REACHED, EXCHANGE MADE?
5022 20DF       0260       JR   NZ,MAIN-$;GO BACK IF EXCHANGE MADE
5024 2A2850     0270       LD   HL,(FIRST);SORT DONE,RESTORE HL
5027 C9         0280       RET  ;EXIT FROM SUBROUTINE
                0290 ;DEFINITIONS
0000            0300 MARK  EQU  0;NAME FOR EXCHANGE MARKER
0002            0310 FIRST DEFS 2;TEMP STORE FIRST ADDRESS
                0320 ;
                0330 ;
```

This produced no errors, so it is a legitimate source program. This does *NOT* mean it will necessarily do what we want, it simply means there are no grammatical errors (as mentioned earlier, there is a logical error in the program which we will discover later).

The print out gives us for each source line in order from left to right:

i. The store location an instruction is stored at
ii. The actual Hex object code
iii. The source line number
iv. Label (if present)
v. The instruction mnemonic or pseudo op code.
vi. Comments (if present)

The reader should check the object code against the tables in the previous chapter to see that the method works! It is also useful in getting a 'feel' for the operation.

We now need to test our routine. Before we can do this we need to discuss the debugging aid known as a "Monitor".

5.6   MONITORS AND BUGS

5.6.1   Introduction

An assembler allows machine code programs to be written, but does not allow them to be run or tested. To do this we need another programming aid known as a Monitor or Bug.

A monitor is a small program (typically $1 - 2K$) that allows the programmer to examine the store and register contents and check a program by stopping it at a strategic point or running a program with a pause between each intruction (known as single stepping).

A monitor can exist in ROM (as does the Nascom NASBUG and NASYS monitors) or be loaded via tape (as the TRS-80 T-BUG). Monitors are often called BUGs because they are used to de-bug a program.

The facilities offered by different monitors vary considerably, but all will have the following (although the terms used may differ). The examples below are for a NASBUG monitor.

5.6.2 Modify

This allows the programmer to examine (and if necessary modify) a store location. If, for example, the programmer wanted to examine location 0C50, he would type:

M 0C50 Newline;

and the computer would reply:

0C50 A5_

meaning location 0C50 contains Hex A5. The programmer can now type in a new value to go into the location. It is thus possible to load a whole machine code program in Hex by the modify command, although it is more usually applied for small corrections.

5.6.3 Execute

This option is used to start a machine code program. The user types E followed by the start location.

E F600 Newline

will execute a machine code program starting at location F600. Note that this is a "Kamikaze" dive into a program, and unlike BASIC could easily corrupt the store if the program contains an error.

5.6.4 Breakpoint

This option stops the program at a pre-determined point and displays the register contents. It is an invaluable aid for fault finding. The breakpoint is set by typing B followed by the locations.

B 1A92 Newline

will set the breakpoint at location 1A92. The register display on a NASBUG is:

SP   PC   AF   HL   DE   BC   I   IX   IY   Flags

103

so a typical display for B1002 could be

    1000   1002 C59A 7C80 817E 7A81 00   234D 0FFE SHN

showing that register A, for example, contains Hex C5.

The usefulness of the breakpoint cannot be overemphasised.

5.6.5   Tabulate

The tabulate function displays the store contents between two specified points, with a NASBUG:

    T 3000 3040 Newline

Could produce

```
>T 3000 3040
  3000 3E 01 0E 05 81 07 FE 1F
  3008 C2 20 30 CD 69 00 DD E1
  3010 30 F7 FE 1F 28 0F DD E5
  3018 CD 3B 01 DD E1 DD 77 00
  3020 DD 23 0C 18 E4 21 00 40
  3028 CD 00 50 21 00 40 41 7E
  3030 CD 3B 01 23 10 F9 18 CB
  3038 FF 00 FF 00 FF 00 FF 00
  >
```

The first few instructions are actually:

```
3000          0010          ORG   £3000
3000 3E01     0020          LD    A,1;ONE IN REGISTER A
3002 0E05     0030          LD    C,5;FIVE IN REGISTER C
3004 81       0040          ADD   A,C;ADD REGISTERS A AND C
3005 07       0050          RLCA ;ROTATE REGISTER A
3006 FE1F     0060          CP    £1F;COMPARE REGISTER A WITH HEX 1F
3008 C22030   0070          JP    NZ,£3020;JUMP TO HEX 3020 IF NON Z
```

which should correspond with the listing.

5.6.6   Single Step

Single step is similar to Execute, except that the computer pauses between each instruction and displays the register contents with the same layout as the breakpoint display. A typical display might be:

104

```
 53000
1000 3002 019A 7C80 817E 7A81 00 1C05 0FFE SHN
>
1000 3004 019A 7C80 817E 7A05 00 1C05 0FFE SHN
>
1000 3005 0600 7C80 817E 7A05 00 1C05 0FFE
>
1000 3006 0C08 7C80 817E 7A05 00 1C05 0FFE
>
1000 3008 0C9B 7C80 817E 7A05 00 1C05 0FFE SHNC
>
1000 3020 0C9B 7C80 817E 7A05 00 1C05 0FFE SHNC
>
1000 3022 0C9B 7C80 817E 7A05 00 1C06 0FFE SHNC
>
```

The above steps are actually the instructions above. The reader should check the register contents against the program at each stage.

5.6.7   Conclusion

The five functions described above are provided on all monitors. Other functions commonly available are write a program to tape or disc, read a program from tape or disc, search for a specified data string, copy data from one part of the store to another. The instruction manuals should be consulted for specific details.

It is possible to write, check and run machine code programs with a monitor only. It is not possible to check machine code programs with just an assembler. Although ideally an assembler and monitor should be obtained, if funds are tight, a monitor alone will suffice.

Some machines (such as the NASCOM) come with a monitor already provided in ROM.

5.7   TESTING A MACHINE CODE PROGRAM

In section 5.5 we wrote a bubble sort subroutine. We will now write a small program to test it. This program will take a series of characters from the keyboard and store them. The characters are then sorted by our subroutine and displayed, sorted, on the VDU screen. Alphanumeric characters are obtained from the keyboard in Hex (A is 41H, B is 42H etc.) so they

105

will be sorted into alphabetical order. The test program can be represented in simple form by the flow chart of Fig.5.3.

Most monitors contain useful subroutines that can be called by the users program. In a NASBUG we have:

i. Keyboard at Hex 0069. This returns with the carry flag set and the Hex code for the character in register A if a key has been pressed. If no key is pressed, the subroutine returns with the carry flag reset.

ii. CRT at Hex 013B. This takes the contents of register A and displays the equivalent character on the VDU.

These two NASBUG routines allow us to produce the detailed flow chart of Fig.5.4 which becomes the source program below:

```
0400 ; TEST PROGRAM FOR BUBBLE SORT
0410 KBD EQU £69; NASBUG KEYBOARD ROUTINE
0420 CRT EQU £13B; NASBUG CRT ROUTINE
0430 SORT EQU £5000; BUBBLE SORT ROUTINE
0440 ;
0450 ORG £3000
0460 LD SP £5FFF; SETUP STACK POINTER
0470 BEG LD C, 0; CLEAR C FOR COUNTER
0480 LD IX, £4000; STRING TO GO FROM 4000
0482 INP PUSH IX; IX USED IN KBD ROUTINE
0490 CALL KBD; GET CHARACTER
0494 POP IX; GET IX BACK AFTER KBD ROUTINE
0500 JR NC INP-$; JUMP BACK NO KEY PRESSED
0510 CP £1F; WAS CHARCTER NEW LINE?
0520 JR Z BUBB-$; IF SO GOTO BUBBLE SORT
0522 PUSH IX; IX USED IN CRT ROUTINE
0530 CALL CRT; DISPLAY CHARACTER
0534 POP IX; GET IX BACK AFTER CRT ROUTINE
0540 LD (IX), A; STORE IT
0550 INC IX; READY FOR NEXT CHARACTER
0560 INC C; INC CHARACTER COUNTER
0570 JR INP-$; GET NEXT CHARACTER
0580 ;
0590 ;
0600 BUBB LD HL, £4000; START ADDRESS OF LIST
0610 CALL SORT
0620 ;
0630 ;
0640 ; DISPLAY SORTED LIST
0650 LD HL, £4000; START OF SORTED LIST
0660 LD B, C; NUMBER IN LIST FOR COUNT
0670 LP LD A, (HL); GET CHARACTER FOR DISPLAY
0680 CALL CRT; AND DISPLAY IT
0690 INC HL; NEXT ADDRESS
0700 DJNZ LP-$; END OF LIST?JUMP BACK IF NO
0710 JR BEG-$; GO BACK FOR ANOTHER LIST
```

Note that the line numbers follow on from the bubble sort routine in section 5.5 so that the subroutine and the test

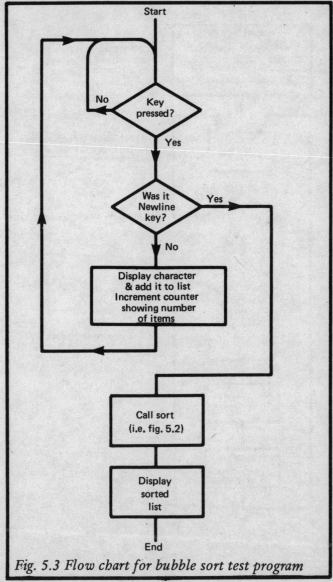

Fig. 5.3 Flow chart for bubble sort test program

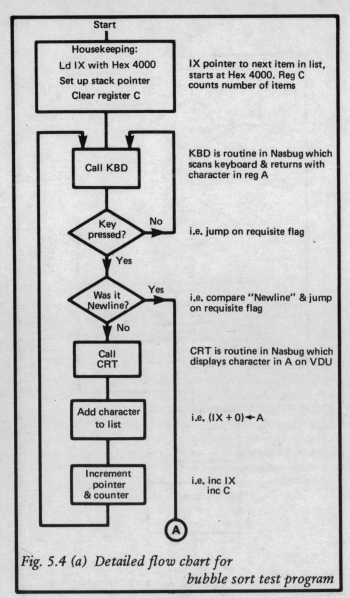

Fig. 5.4 (a) Detailed flow chart for
bubble sort test program

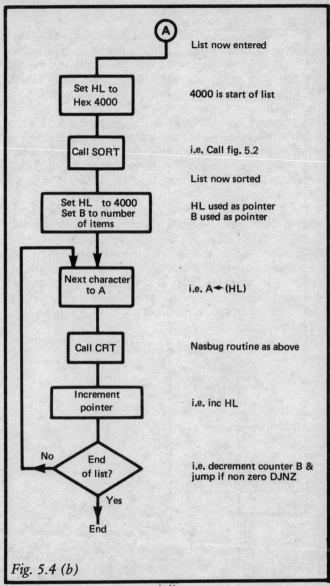

Fig. 5.4 (b)

program can be assembled together.

The program is relatively straightforward. The input portion occupies lines 400 − 570 and the output portion lines 640 − 710. Between these we call the bubble sort routine. The first lines define the labels KBD and CRT to call the NASBUG routines and say where the test program is to go (Hex 3000).

A character is obtained from the keyboard at lines 482 − 500, and stored using indexed addressing in locations from 540. Register C is used to count how many characters have been input. When a newline character is detected, the bubble sort routine is called. A typed character is displayed at line 530.

The output routine works up the sorted list using register indirect addressing, sending characters to the Nasbug CRT routine to display them. Register B is used as a counter.

The test program and routine are assembled together, and the assembler directed to load the resulting object program to store and to tape (the latter as a precaution in the not unlikely event that a programming error causes the computer to crash. Remember, unlike BASIC, a machine code program can self destruct). We now have:

```
                0010 ;*** BUBBLE SORT ROUTINE ***
                0020 ;ENTER WITH FIRST ITEM ADDRESS IN HL
                0030 ;NUMBER OF ITEMS IN C (2 TO 255)
                0040 ;EXIT WITH:
                0050 ;ITEMS SORTED IN SAME STORE BLOCK
                0060 ;HL AND C UNCHANGED
                0070 ;REGISTERS A B E IX USED
                0080 ;OTHER REGISTERS UNCHANGED
                0090 ;
5000            0100 SORT    ORG   £5000;ADDRESS FOR ROUTINE
5000 222850     0110         LD    (FIRST),HL;SAVE ADDRESS TO FREE H
5003 CB84       0120 MAIN    RES   MARK,H;CLEAR EXCHANGE MARKER
5005 41         0130         LD    B,C;SET UP COUNTER FOR TESTS
5006 05         0140         DEC   B;COMPARISONS 1 LESS THAN ITEMS
5007 DD2A2850   0150         LD    IX,(FIRST);SET IX TO START OF LIST
500B DD7E00     0160 NEXT    LD    A,(IX+0);GET FIRST OF PAIR
500E DD5E01     0170         LD    E,(IX+1);GET SECOND OF PAIR
5011 BB         0180         CP    E;COMPARE THEM
5012 3008       0190         JR    NC NOEX-$;EXCHANGE NEEDED?
5014 DD7300     0200         LD    (IX+0),E;YES, PUT BACK EXCHANGED
5017 DD7701     0210         LD    (IX+1),A;DITTO
501A CBC4       0220         SET   MARK,H;MARKER SHOWS EXCHANGE MADE
501C DD23       0230 NOEX    INC   IX;SET IX FOR NEXT PAIR
501E 10EB       0240         DJNZ  NEXT-$;JUMP BACK IF NOT END LIST
5020 CB44       0250         BIT   MARK,H;END REACHED,EXCHANGE MADE?
5022 20DF       0260         JR    NZ,MAIN-$;GO BACK IF EXCHANGE MADE
5024 2A2850     0270         LD    HL,(FIRST);SORT DONE,RESTORE HL
```

110

```
5027 C9        0280        RET  ;EXIT FROM SUBROUTINE
               0290 ;DEFINITIONS
0000           0300 MARK   EQU  0;NAME FOR EXCHANGE MARKER
0002           0310 FIRST  DEFS 2;TEMP STORE FIRST ADDRESS
               0320 ;
               0330 ;
               0340 ;
               0350 ;
               0360 ;
               0370 ;
               0380 ;
               0390 ;
               0400 ;TEST PROGRAM FOR BUBBLE SORT
0069           0410 KBD    EQU  £69;NASBUG KEYBOARD ROUTINE
013B           0420 CRT    EQU  £13B;NASBUG CRT ROUTINE
               0430 ;
               0440 ;
3000           0450        ORG  £3000
3000 31FF5F    0460        LD   SP £5FFF;SETUP STACK POINTER
3003 0E00      0470 BEG    LD   C,0;CLEAR C FOR COUNTER
3005 DD210040  0480        LD   IX,£4000;STRING TO GO FROM 4000
3009 DDE5      0482 INP    PUSH IX;IX USED IN KBD ROUTINE
300B CD6900    0490        CALL KBD;GET CHARACTER
300E DDE1      0494        POP  IX;GET IX BACK AFTER KBD ROUTINE
3010 30F7      0500        JR   NC INP-$;JUMP BACK FOR NO KEY PRESSED
3012 FE1F      0510        CP   £1F;HAS CHARCTER NEW LINE?
3014 280F      0520        JR   Z BUBB-$;IF SO GOTO BUBBLE SORT
3016 DDE5      0522        PUSH IX;IX USED IN CRT ROUTINE
3018 CD3B01    0530        CALL CRT;DISPLAY CHARACTER
301B DDE1      0534        POP  IX;GET IX BACK AFTER CRT ROUTINE
301D DD7700    0540        LD   (IX),A;STORE IT
3020 DD23      0550        INC  IX;READY FOR NEXT CHARACTER
3022 0C        0560        INC  C;INC CHARACTER COUNTER
3023 18E4      0570        JR   INP-$;GET NEXT CHARACTER
               0580 ;
               0590 ;
3025 210040    0600 BUBB   LD   HL,£4000;START ADDRESS OF LIST
3028 CD0050    0610        CALL SORT
               0620 ;
               0630 ;
               0640 ;DISPLAY SORTED LIST
302B 210040    0650        LD   HL,£4000;START OF SORTED LIST
302E 41        0660        LD   B,C;NUMBER IN LIST FOR COUNT
302F 7E        0670 LP     LD   A,(HL);GET CHARACTER FOR DISPLAY
3030 CD3B01    0680        CALL CRT;AND DISPLAY IT
3033 23        0690        INC  HL;NEXT ADDRESS
3034 10F9      0700        DJNZ LP-$;END OF LIST?JUMP BACK IF NO
3036 18CB      0710        JR   BEG-$;GO BACK FOR ANOTHER LIST
```

To run this, we call up the monitor and type E3000 to
enter our test program. As expected we get the VDU prompt
from the KBD routine. Full of optimism we type:

QWERTYUIOP Newline

and on the screen comes:

EIOPRTUQWY

WHICH IS WHAT WE WOULD EXPECT. We now try:

111

Nothing happens. The computer does not reply with a sorted string (or for that matter anything). Our logical bug has surfaced.

Examining the store with the monitor tabulate function shows the store to be uncorrupted. The program is run again with the breakpoint set for the first location in the output portion of the test program (i.e. B 302B). Running the program again, we find that the breakpoint is not reached; the bubble sort routine is tied up in a permanently running loop.

Further checks with the breakpoint shows that the bubble sort routine does not work correctly where there are duplicate characters. As written it will sort D F A X Y but not D F F A X Y. In the original source program, the test at line 190 not only exchanges numbers that are out of order, but also exchanges numbers that are the same. A list with duplicates will therefore never finish; the routine will continue for ever interchanging the duplicates!

This can easily be cured. If we add a line 195, to the source program to jump to NOEX if the characters are the same, the routine will not run for ever with duplicate numbers. The assembler is instructed to re-assemble the source program, (and takes care of all the new locations and relative jumps).

```
                    0010 ;*** BUBBLE SORT ROUTINE ***
                    0020 ;ENTER WITH FIRST ITEM ADDRESS IN HL
                    0030 ;NUMBER OF ITEMS IN C (2 TO 255)
                    0040 ;EXIT WITH:
                    0050 ;ITEMS SORTED IN SAME STORE BLOCK
                    0060 ;HL AND C UNCHANGED
                    0070 ;REGISTERS A B E IX USED
                    0080 ;OTHER REGISTERS UNCHANGED
                    0090 ;
5000                0100 SORT   ORG  £5000;ADDRESS FOR ROUTINE
5000 222A50         0110        LD   (FIRST),HL;SAVE ADDRESS TO FREE H
5003 CB84           0120 MAIN   RES  MARK,H;CLEAR EXCHANGE MARKER
5005 41             0130        LD   B,C;SET UP COUNTER FOR TESTS
5006 05             0140        DEC  B;COMPARISONS 1 LESS THAN ITEMS
5007 DD2A2A50       0150        LD   IX,(FIRST);SET IX TO START OF LIST
500B DD7E00         0160 NEXT   LD   A,(IX+0);GET FIRST OF PAIR
500E DD5E01         0170        LD   E,(IX+1);GET SECOND OF PAIR
5011 BB             0180        CP   E;COMPARE THEM
5012 300A           0190        JR   NC NOEX-$;NO EXCHANGE IF CORRECT
5014 2808           0195        JR   Z NOEX-$;NO EXCHANGE IF SAME
5016 DD7300         0200        LD   (IX+0),E;EXCHANGE NEEDED SO SWAP
5019 DD7701         0210        LD   (IX+1),A;THE TWO CHARACTERS
501C CBC4           0220        SET  MARK,H;MARKER SHOWS EXCHANGE MADE
501E DD23           0230 NOEX   INC  IX;SET IX FOR NEXT PAIR
```

```
5020 10E9    0240         DJNZ NEXT-$; JUMP BACK IF NOT END LIST
5022 CB44    0250         BIT  MARK, H; END REACHED, EXCHANGE MADE?
5024 20DD    0260         JR   NZ, MAIN-$; GO BACK IF EXCHANGE MADE
5026 2A2A50  0270         LD   HL, (FIRST); SORT DONE, RESTORE HL
5029 C9      0280         RET  ; EXIT FROM SUBROUTINE
             0290 ; DEFINITIONS
0000         0300 MARK    EQU  0; NAME FOR EXCHANGE MARKER
0002         0310 FIRST   DEFS 2; TEMP STORE FIRST ADDRESS
             0320 ;
             0330 ;
```

The resulting program is tested as before. This time:

THE QUICK BROWN FOX   Newline

gives:

BCEFHIKNOOQRTUWX

Note the four spaces come at the start of the sorted list.

5.8   CONCLUSION

The writing and testing of our bubble test program should
serve to show the basics of assembly language programming.
There are dialect variations between different assemblers,
so it is advisable to check carefully how individual assemblers
and monitors differ from those described above.

A bubble sort is rather an inefficient way of sorting, and
the routine above has been written for ease of comprehension
rather than speed or elegance. It would be a useful exercise for
the reader to consider how faster sort routines could be
implemented.

Chapter Six

INTERFACING THE Z-80

6.1 INTRODUCTION

To be useful, a computer must be able to communicate with the outside world. At the simplest level we need to be able to input from a keyboard and cassette recorder, and output to a TV screen and tape recorder. More ambitious systems will have printers, discs and possible control external items such as laboratory experiments or industrial plant.

In this chapter we will describe how the Z-80 communicates with its external devices.

6.2 SERIAL AND PARALLEL COMMUNICATION

All communication between micros and the outside world takes place in the form of 8 bit words. If the data is alpha-numeric, the 8 bits will usually represent a character in the ASCII code (see Appendix C). If the data is used in instrumentation the 8 bits will represent the value of a variable such as temperatures or pressure. If the data is being used for control, individual bits in the word will be used to represent the states of limit switches, valves, lamps etc.

If we are to send 8 bit words from place to place, there are two methods we can use. In Fig. 6.1a we simply send the data down 8 wires simultaneously. This is known as parallel transmission and is (in essence) the method used inside a microcomputer. It can, of course, be used to transmit data outside the computer.

In Fig. 6.1b the data is sent as a serial pulse train down a single wire. This is known as serial transmission. Obviously, serial transmission is slower, but cheaper, than parallel transmission.

Internally, all data movement in a microcomputer is done in parallel. I/O ports therefore communicate with the

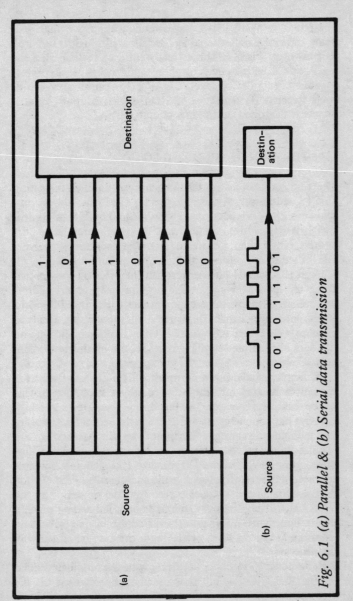

Fig. 6.1 (a) Parallel & (b) Serial data transmission

computer in parallel. If serial communication is being used, some form of parallel/serial and serial/parallel logic is required as shown on Fig.6.2. This is really little more than an 8 bit shift register with some control logic. Fig. 6.2 is usually implemented with a device called a UART (for Universal Synchronous Receiver Transmitter) or SIO (for Serial Input Output). These are described further in section 6.6.

6.3 PORT ADDRESSING AND LOGIC

The fundamentals of port addressing was outlined in section 1.5. I/O addressing is done via bits $0 - 7$ of the address bus, allowing 256 port addresses in the range $0 - 255$. A control signal IORQ is used to indicate that an address is a port address rather than a store address. The data direction signal RD is used to indicate whether an input or output is required.

A simple parallel output port can therefore be constructed along the lines of Fig. 6.3. The bottom 8 bits of the address bus are decoded by some logic decoder (such as a 74138) to give a port select signal. This is gated with the timing signals to produce a clock signal for the 8 D types flip flops. The data on the data bus is stored in the D types for use by the device connected to the port.

A simple parallel input port is shown on Fig.6.4. Data from the device is gated into the 8 D types by a strobe signal. This strobe can be generated by the device itself (e.g. an ADC saying it has completed its digitisation (see Section 6.9)) or by the computer wanting a 'snapshot' of the port state (e.g. reading limit switch states on an industrial control application). This loading of the D types can take place at any time and need not necessarily involve the computer.

The state of the D types is read into the processor by the rest of the logic. The port address is decoded and gated with the timing signals to enable the 8 tristate buffers. The data from the D types is then available on the data bus for use by the processor.

It is possible to construct ports with discrete logic similar to Figs. 6.3 and 6.4, but it is usually simpler to use the ICs

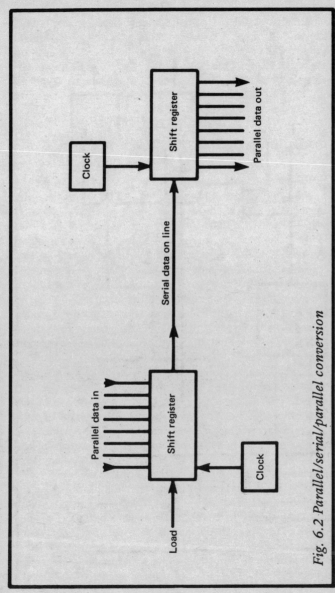

Fig. 6.2 Parallel/serial/parallel conversion

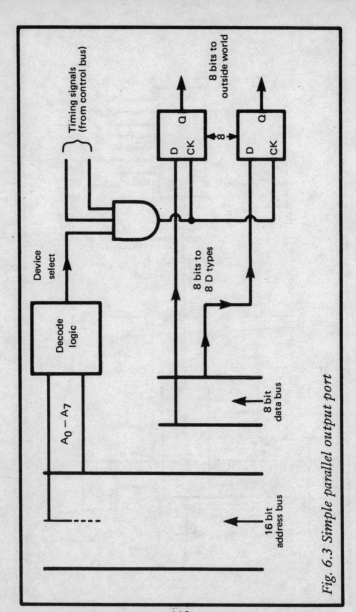

Fig. 6.3 Simple parallel output port

118

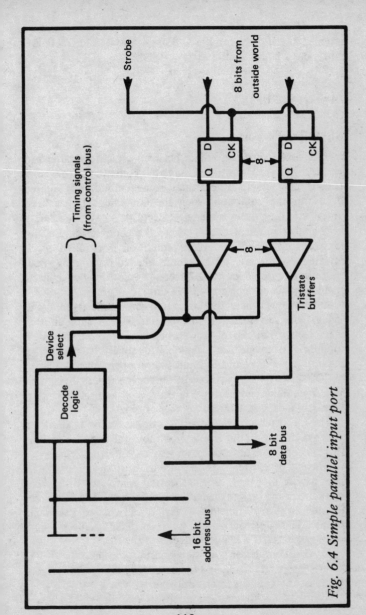

Fig. 6.4 Simple parallel input port

119

designed specifically for the I/O applications. The Z-80 PIO chip is described in section 6.5.

6.4 INTERRUPTS

6.4.1 Introduction

There is a vast speed difference between a microcomputer and even a high speed printer. If, say, the computer is to send a string of characters to the printer, some method must be used to inform the computer when the last character has been printed and the printer is ready to accept the next character.

A similar problem occurs where the computer is used for control purposes. If an alarm condition is required to be detected within, say, 0.2 seconds the corresponding input must be monitored every 0.2 seconds even though the alarm might only occur once every five years.

A technique where the computer goes round its inputs at regular intervals seeing if the printer is ready for another character or an alarm condition has occurred is called "polling". Although it is acceptable for small systems, polling ties up the processor in unnecessary operations. In larger systems it may be impossible to obtain the required response time by polling, as the time taken to poll and service inputs obviously increases with the number of inputs.

The ideal solution would allow a device requiring attention to signal directly to the processor without the need for polling. This is known, for obvious reasons, as an "interrupt".

When a device requires the attention of the processor, it requests an interrupt. The processor completes its current instruction and acknowledges the interrupt. The processor now identifies the interrupting device, and goes to a servicing routine. This is performed in a similar manner to a normal sub-routine, with the PC being pushed onto the stack.

At the completion of the servicing routine, the PC is restored from the stack, and the main program continues from the point at which the interrupt occurred.

Normally an interrupt hierarchy is established to allow a

more urgent interrupt to interrupt a lower priority servicing routine. A typical sequence of events is shown on Fig. 6.5.

6.4.2 Servicing an Interrupt

There are basically three different ways of responding to an interrupt, but all have the same objective of identifying the device initiating the interrupt, and calling the servicing routine.

The simplest method, used on early microprocessors, has a common interrupt servicing routine. When an interrupt occurs, this common routine polls all the devices ("who said that?") and then calls the correct servicing routine.

The 8080 uses a more elegant method. When the processor has pushed the PC onto the stack it acknowledges the interrupt request and releases control of the data bus. The interrupting device now forces an instruction onto the bus which is almost always a subroutine call to its servicing routine. The RST instructions (see section 4.9) are particularly useful for this purpose.

The Z-80 can use the simple "who said that" method, the 8080 method (for compatability) and a powerful method of its own. The flexibility and sophistication of its interrupt handling is one of the Z-80's best features.

The Z-80's own method uses the 8 bit 'I' register. This contains the top 8 bits of a store address. When an interrupt is acknowledged, the device supplies the bottom 8 bits. The 16 bits together indicate two store locations which contain the address of the servicing subroutine. This operation sounds more complex than it actually is, and possibly is best summarised by Fig.6.6. The I register actually designates an area of store to be used as a table to hold the addresses of the interrupt service routine.

6.4.3 Z-80 Interrupts

The Z-80 can handle interrupts in three different ways, called, not surprisingly, Mode 0, Mode 1, Mode 2. The mode is selected by control instructions (see table 4.15). The mnemonics for these are 'IM0', 'IM1', 'IM2'. Only one

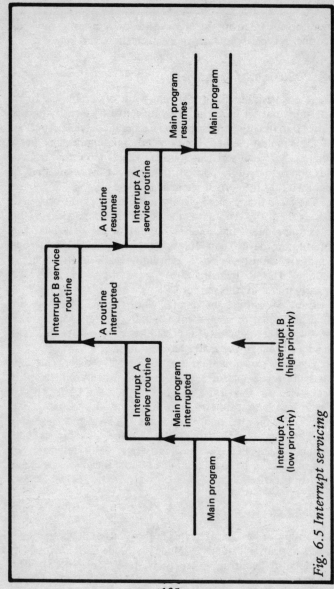

Fig. 6.5 Interrupt servicing

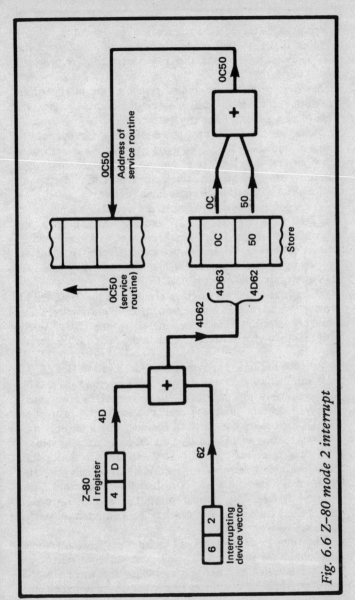

Fig. 6.6 Z-80 mode 2 interrupt

interrupt mode can be used at once.

Mode 0 is the 8080 mode. On receipt of an interrupt the Z-80 releases the data bus, then obeys an instruction provided by the device.

Mode 1 is the simple polled response. On receipt of an interrupt the processor calls a subroutine located at Hex 38. This address is "built into" the instruction.

Mode 2 is the Z-80's own powerful mode, and operates as outlined above. It should be apparent that the programmer must ensure the I register and address table are loaded correctly. We shall see in later sections how the interrupting device obtains its half of the data table address.

The interrupts described above are detected via pin 16 of the Z-80 CPU chip (see Fig.2.7 and section 2.3). These are known as Maskable Interrupts because the programmer can enable or disable the processors response. This is achieved by two control instructions; Enable Interrupt '(EI)', and Disable Interrupts '(DI)'. (See table 4.15).

There is also another interrupt facility on the Z-80. Pin 17 provides a non maskable interrupt. As its name implies, a non maskable interrupt cannot be ignored by the CPU. Usually NMI is used for interrupt functions such as powerfail detection.

An NMI has only one response mode, a call to Hex 66. An NMI automatically disables the maskable interrupts to prevent its (presumably top priority) routine from being interrupted. A special "return from non maskable interrupt" instruction ('REIN') reinstates the status of the maskable interrupts after the NMI routine whilst returning the PC to its previous value.

Return from maskable interrupts should use the "return from maskable interrupt" instruction (RETI). This reinstates PC from the stack and allows further interrupts from lower priority devices. The normal subroutine return instruction (RET) should not be used to return from an interrupt service routine.

The timing and operation of an interrupt is shown, somewhat simplified form, on Fig. 6.7. The sequence starts by a device requesting an interrupt by pulling the wired OR INT line low. The CPU completes its current instruction then pulls

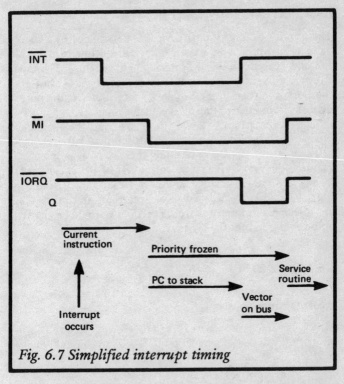

Fig. 6.7 Simplified interrupt timing

MI low. This freezes the priority status, preventing further interrupts tripping over each other during the short time whilst the PC is put on the stack. After PC is put onto the stack, IORQ is taken low which signals to the device that the low byte for the address table is required. When this is provided the CPU jumps to the address provided by the table. IORQ and MI go back high and the service routine is being obeyed. The priority is unfrozen and further interrupts can take place. The interrupting device watches the data bus for a RETI instruction signifying the end of the service routine. When this occurs the device then allows interrupts from lower priority devices on the daisy chain.

6.4.4 INTERRUPT PRIORITY

The priority of interrupting devices is determined by a simple daisy chain. Each port has an input called "Interrupt Enable In" and an output called "Interrupt Enable Out". The input allows the port to signal an interrupt. The output indicates if the port is currently engaged in an interrupt *OR* the port is disabled from interrupting by the enable input.

"Enable interrupt" is high to enable, and the "Interrupt Enable Out" signal is low when the port is disabled or engaged in an interrupt. By daisy chaining these signals, as shown on Fig. 6.8, the priority increases to the left of the chain, port 6 having the highest priority, and port 1 the lowest. As drawn, port 4 is currently engaged in an interrupt, and ports 1,2,3 are disabled. An interrupt from port 5 or 6 would be allowed, and would interrupt the service routine for port 4.

6.5 THE Z-80 PIO

6.5.1 Introduction

Most microprocessor manufacturers provide special IC's to simplify the design of parallel ports. The Z-80 chip is known as a PIO (for parallel input output, what else?) and gives the user two 8 bit ports which can be configured to be input ports, output ports or bidirectional. Interrupt logic is also included.

A block diagram of the Z-80 PIO is shown on Fig. 6.9. The PIO connects to the CPU via the usual address, data and control highways. External logic is required to decode the PIO address and select the chip via the chip enable input. We will describe the other control signals later.

The two ports are known as A and B. The ports can be used in four modes.

i. Input, 8 bit input port with full handshake
ii. Output, 8 bit output with full handshake
iii. Bidirectional (port A only). The port responds to both input and output commands. This mode is used where

126

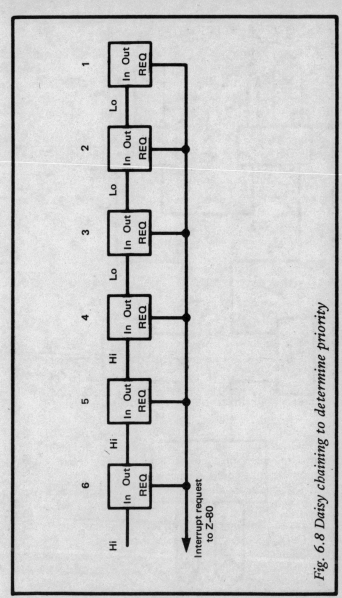

Fig. 6.8 Daisy chaining to determine priority

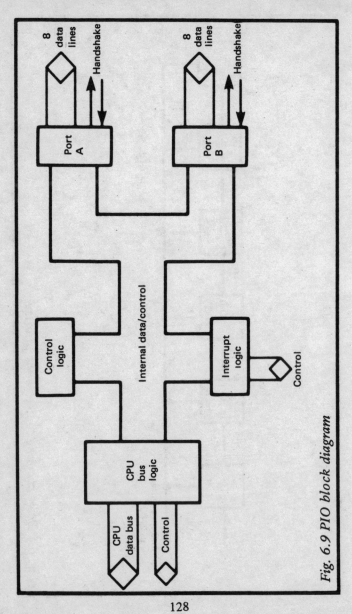

Fig. 6.9 PIO block diagram

128

the PIO feeds onto an external I/O bus in, for example, data logging applications. Full handshake is provided.

iv. Bit mode. The user specifies which bits in a port are to be inputs and which are to be outputs. These bits then respond respectively to input and output commands. No handshaking is provided.

Interrupts can be generated on inputs or on the successful completion of an output. The "interrupt request" signal is given by an open collector output to give the single "interrupt request" to the processor. "Interrupt Enable" and "Interrupt in progress" operate as above.

Before the PIO can be used, therefore, the user has to perform a considerable setting up operation. Briefly, the user must specify for both A and B ports:

i. The operating mode (as above)
ii. If Bit Mode is selected, which bits are inputs and which are outputs.
iii. If interrupts are to be used
iv. The interrupt conditions
v. The interrupt table address low byte, known as the interrupt vector (see sections 6.4.2 and 6.4.3)

This information is loaded into the PIO at the start of the users program.

The PIO must obviously need to distinguish between set up data and data to be sent to the outside world. This is achieved by a control signal called "C/D select". If this is high during an output command, the data on the data bus is interpreted as set up data in a manner described later. If the C/D select is low during an output command, the data on the data bus is passed onto the outside world.

The PIO also needs to be told if an input or output command is for the A port or the B port. A control signal called "A/B select" is provided for this purpose. If this input is high, port A is being used. If the input is low, port B is select.

It is usual to connect A/B select to bit A0 on the address bus and C/D select to bit A1 on the address bus, and decode bits A2 to A7 to select the PIO via the chip enable. On

Fig.6.10 the chip is selected when A2 is high and A3 — A7 are low. The PIO then uses four addresses as below:

4	Port B	data transfer
5	Port A	data transfer
6	Port B	set up data
7	Port A	set up data

6.5.2 Set Up Data

The PIO must be initialised before any data can be transferred. This involves several stages. First, an operating mode must be defined for port A and B. This is done by sending a control word for each port with the format in Fig.6.11.

Bits D0 to D3 define that a mode is being selected, and bits D6, D7 define the mode. Bits D4, D5 are unused and are conventionally reset. We therefore have:

M1	M0	Hex	Mode
0	0	0F	output
0	1	4F	input
1	0	8F	bidirectional
1	1	FF	bit

The instructions to set port A to be an input port would therefore be (for the PIO in Fig.6.10)

LD A £4F ; 4F is the code for input mode
OUT 7 ; Port 7 set up for port A

When the bit mode is selected, a second set up word must be sent to define which bits are to be inputs and which are outputs. A '1' means that the corresponding data bit will be used as an input. If, for example, we sent:

1 0 1 1 0 0 1 1 (Hex B3)
Bits 0, 1, 4, 5 and 7 are inputs
Bits 2, 3 and 6 are outputs

To set up a bit mode operation with the above pattern we would write

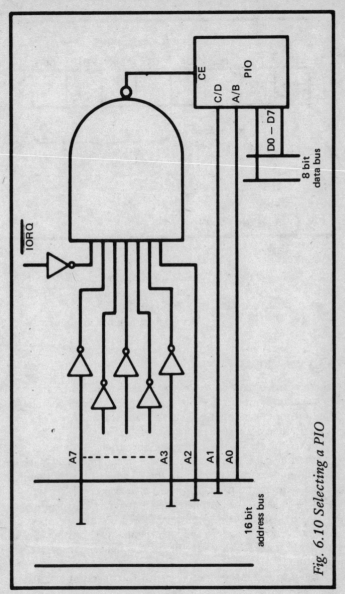

Fig. 6.10 Selecting a PIO

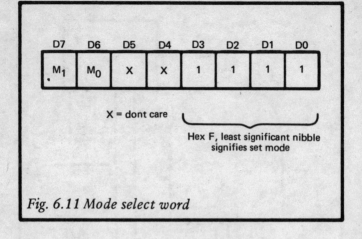

Fig. 6.11 Mode select word

```
LD A, £FF ;   Code for Bit Mode
OUT 7      ;   Port 7 set up for port A
LD A, £B3 ;   Directional data
OUT 7      ;   Set up direction of data lines
```

6.5.3   Handshaking

There are two handshake lines with each port. Those are used to generate an interrupt when an output has been completed (output mode) an input is requested (input mode) or a specific bit pattern appears at the port as data.

Fig. 6.12 shows the timing for an output. At point A the composite WR* signal goes low to signal that new data is present and can be latched into the PIO. Shortly after the PIO changes the port output, WR* goes high again, and Ready goes high to signal to the peripheral device that new data is present. (point B). When the device has accepted the data it takes the strobe line low (point D) and high (point E). This rising edge is used by the PIO to clear the Ready line and generate an interrupt.

Input timing is shown on Fig.6.13. This operation is initiated

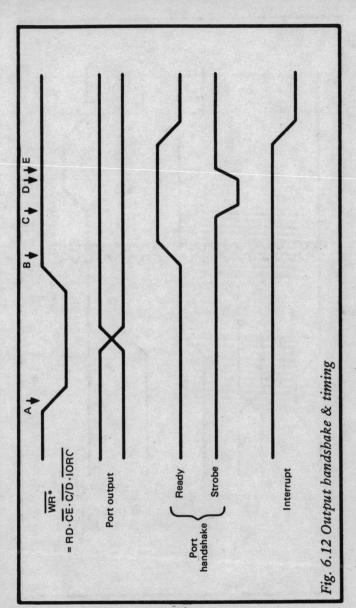

$\overline{WR}^*$

$= RD \cdot \overline{CE} \cdot \overline{C/D} \cdot \overline{IORC}$

Port output

Ready

Strobe

Port
handshake

Interrupt

Fig. 6.12 Output handshake & timing

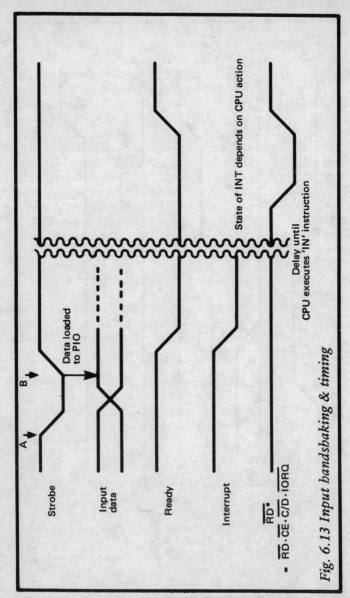

Fig. 6.13 Input handshaking & timing

by the peripheral device which presents data to the input port and takes the strobe line low. This latches the data into the PIO. The rising edge of the strobe (point B) causes the Ready line to go low and an interrupt to be generated. When the CPU reads from the port, the composite signal RD* is generated inside the PIO, and the rising edge of this takes Ready high to signal to the peripheral device that another input can be made.

Bidirectional operation is simply a combination of input and output operation, but suffers from the restriction of a 40 pin chip. Bidirectional operation requires four handshake lines, two for input and two for output. Pin limitation means that only two handshake lines are provided per port. Bidirectional operation is therefore only available on port A, with port A handshakes used for the outputs, and port B handshakes for the inputs. Port B itself must be used in the bit mode which does not use handshaking. Care must obviously be taken with the peripheral device logic to ensure that it is not writing to a bidirectional port whilst the CPU is performing an output.

In bit mode, no handshaking is used. Data output from the CPU appears at the port output. An input from the port takes a "snapshot" of the inputs. The current state of output lines are read along with the input. Interrupts are generated on the presence of a predetermined bit pattern as described in the section following.

It should be noted that Figs.6.12 and 6.13, whilst adequate for most purposes, are slightly simplified in that the relationship to the clock signal are ignored. For full timing details the Z-80 PIO Technical Manual should be consulted.

6.5.4 Interrupts

To use interrupts in the PIO we must set up the interrupt vector (see section 6.4.3). This is done by writing a set up word with the format of Fig.6.14. Bit 0 being a zero indicates that this set up data is an interrupt vector. The low byte of the table address is always zero.

If, for example, the I register in the Z-80 contained Hex 1D, and the user wrote to the PIO the set up word C4, the service address for the PIO would be found in location 1DC4

135

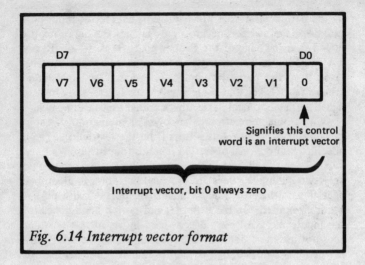

Fig. 6.14 Interrupt vector format

and 1DC5.

If input, output or bidirectional modes are being used, interrupts are generated automatically by the handshaking (see above). In the bit mode, an interrupt will be generated if a previously specified bit pattern occurs.

To do this, we first send an interrupt control word as Fig.6.15. Bits 0 – 3 indicate that this is an interrupt control word. Bit 7 is used to enable and disable interrupts (1 to enable, 0 to disable). This control interrupts in all modes (input, output, bidirectional and bit). Bits 4–6 are only relevant in the bit mode. We will shortly be sending a bit pattern to indicate which bits we want to monitor for an interrupt. Bit 6 indicates if an interrupt is to be generated if *ANY* of the specified bits is present (called OR) or when *ALL* are present called (AND). If Bit 6 is a '1' the AND operation is specified.

Bit 5 is used to indicate if the data lines are to be used to generate an interrupt when they are a '0' or a '1'. If bit 5 is a '1', interrupts will be generated when the specified bits go to a '1', if bit 5 is an '0', interrupts will be generated when the specified bits go to a '0'.

If bit 4 is a '1', the next set up word *MUST* be a mask. A '0'

136

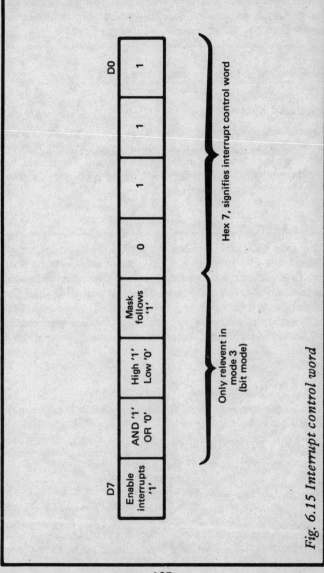

Fig. 6.15 Interrupt control word

in this word means that the corresponding bit will be checked for generating an input in accordance with the conditions set up via Fig.6.15. If, for example, we sent the mask:

$$0 1 1 0 0 0 1 1$$

we would check for interrupts on bits 2, 3, 4 and 7.

6.5.5 Set Up Summary

The procedure for setting up a PIO at first sight seems rather involved. Fig.6.16 shows the procedure in flow chart form, and hopefully will make the matter clearer. It should be remembered that usually only one set up is needed, and this should be placed at the start of the program.

6.5.6 Power Up Problems

At power up, the PIO sets itself into a reset state. Usually, though, the PIO seems to end up in some indeterminate state due to glitches as the supplies come up. Often the PIO seems to set itself into the condition where it is expecting interrupt mask or a data direction word for mode 3. To be certain that a PIO is correctly initialised, a dummy set up data word should be sent to each port before following the procedure in Fig.6.16.

6.5.7 Pinning

The PIO pin connections are shown on Fig.6.17. These operate as below:

   i. D0 – D7 Tristate Data Bus
  ii. A/B Select. A low selects port A, a high selects port B. Usually connected to Address Bus A0.
 iii. C/D Select. Determines whether data on the data bus is to be used as set up data, or port data. A high indicates that set up data is present. Usually connected to A1.
  iv. $\overline{CE}$ Chip enable. Low to select the chip. Usually derived from external decoding logic connected to the address bus.

138

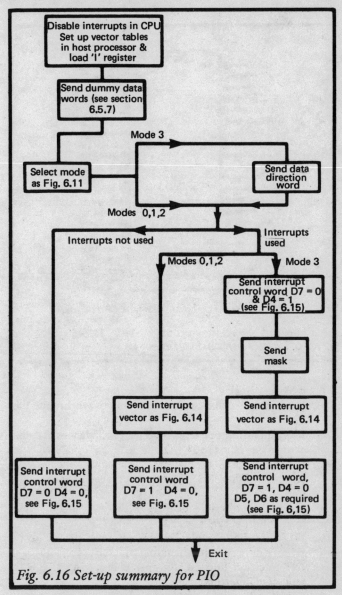

Fig. 6.16 Set-up summary for PIO

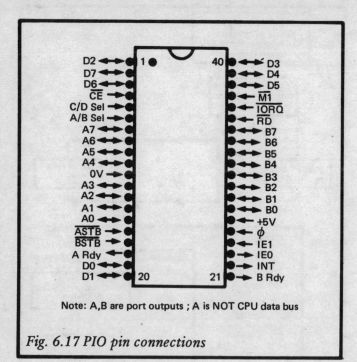

Note: A,B are port outputs ; A is NOT CPU data bus

Fig. 6.17 PIO pin connections

   v. ϕ System clock.

  vi. M1 Timing signal from the CPU used to synchronise the PIO.

 vii. $\overline{\text{IORQ}}$ Input/output request. When low indicates that the address bus refers to an I/O port.

viii. $\overline{\text{RD}}$ Read. Used to indicate if an input or output is requested. When $\overline{\text{RD}}$ is low an input is required from the port.

  ix. IEI Interrupt Enable In. Part of the daisy chain. When high, interrupts are allowed.

   x. IEO Interrupt Enable Out. When low, blocks lower priority devices from generating an interrupt.

  xi. INT Interrupt Request. An open collector signal, low to request an interrupt.

xii. A0 – A7, B0 – B7. Data connections to outside world.

xiii. $\overline{\text{A STB}}$, $\overline{\text{B STB}}$. Strobe signals for handshake *FROM* peripheral device.

xiv. A READY, B READY. Handshake signals *TO* peripheral device.

The PIO requires a single 5V supply at 100mA.

6.6   SERIAL COMMUNICATION & UARTS

6.6.1   Introduction

Serial outputs are commonly used to communicate with printers and other peripherals. Because a computer internally works in parallel, a serial port must incorporate parallel/serial and serial/parallel conversion logic as outlined in section 6.2. This is usually achieved with a special chip called a UART (Universal Asynchronous Receiver Transmitter). The Z-80 UART is also known as an SIO (for Serial Input Output). Although described for outputs from a computer, the circuits described are, of course, also used to input data serially from a peripheral.

6.6.2   Signals and Standards

Before we can describe how a UART works, we must first establish how a serial signal is transmitted. Although there are several different transmissions standards (V24, RS232, 20mA) the actual data format used is the same as Fig.6.18 regardless of the standard used.

When no signal is being sent, the line is a '1'. The first bit is a '0' to indicate the start of a character. The data now follows, seven or eight bits according to the peripheral used. The data is followed by a parity bit. The end of the character is indicated by one (or two) '1' bits (known as the stop bit(s)). Depending on the system, the word length and the number of stop bits, nine to twelve bits can be used to transmit a single character.

A UART is therefore required to convert 8 bit data from

the computer to the serial format of Fig.6.18.

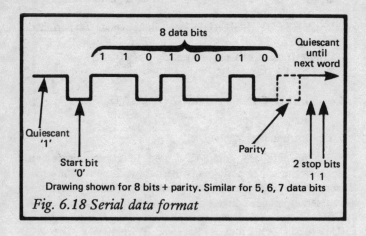

Fig. 6.18 Serial data format

6.6.3 UARTs

In describing a UART, a small problem becomes apparent. The Z-80 family contains a UART (called a SIO) but this is a relatively new device, rather sophisticated (being designed for modems) and a wee bit expensive. Most Z-80 based microcomputers therefore use the cheaper and less sophisticated 6402 UART which has become an industry standard. It was therefore decided to describe the 6402 in detail rather than the Z-80 SIO.

The UART block diagram is shown on Fig.6.19. Because a UART handles both transmitted and received data it has independent transmit and receive sections. These are linked by common control logic which selects the operating mode (i.e. the number of data bits, the parity sign, the number of stop bits). The mode is selected by the five inputs CLS2, CLS1, PI, EPE, SBS in accordance with Table 6.1. These will be hardwired, and are not normally selected by the processor.

The transmitter section is simplest and will be described first. Data is loaded into a data buffer when TBRL (transmitter buffer load) goes low. When TBRL goes high, the output

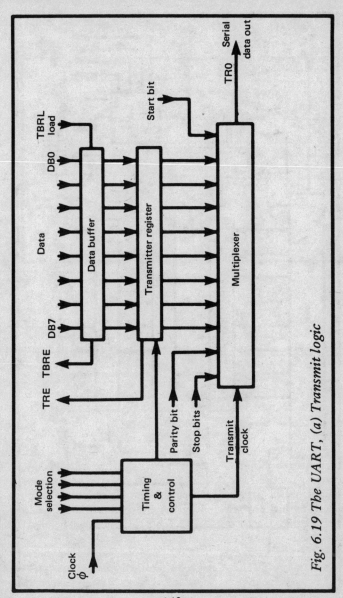

Fig. 6.19 The UART, (a) Transmit logic

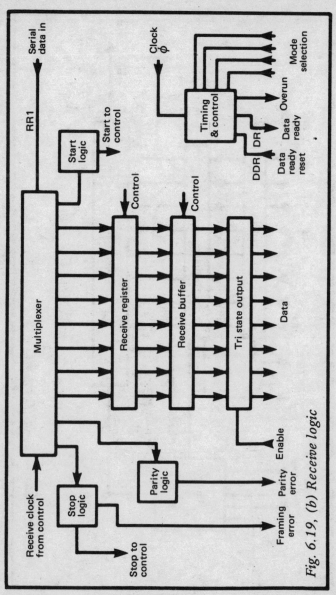

Fig. 6.19, (b) Receive logic

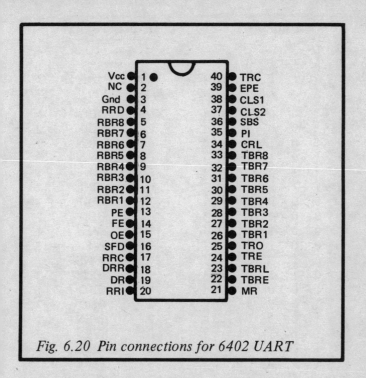

Fig. 6.20 Pin connections for 6402 UART

Table 6.1 Mode Selection for 6402 UART

CONTROL WORD					CHARACTER FORMAT			
C L S 2	C L S 1	P I	E P E	S B S	START BIT	DATA BITS	PARITY BIT	STOP BITS
0	0	0	0	0	1	5	ODD	1
0	0	0	0	1	1	5	ODD	1.5
0	0	0	1	0	1	5	EVEN	1
0	0	0	1	1	1	5	EVEN	1.5
0	0	1	X	0	1	5	NONE	1
0	0	1	X	1	1	5	NONE	1.5

CONTROL WORD					CHARACTER FORMAT			
C L S 2	C L S 1	P I	E P E	S B S	START BIT	DATA BITS	PARITY BIT	STOP BITS
0	1	0	0	0	1	6	ODD	1
0	1	0	0	1	1	6	ODD	2
0	1	0	1	0	1	6	EVEN	1
0	1	0	1	1	1	6	EVEN	2
0	1	1	X	0	1	6	NONE	1
0	1	1	X	1	1	6	NONE	2
1	0	0	0	0	1	7	ODD	1
1	0	0	0	1	1	7	ODD	2
1	0	0	1	0	1	7	EVEN	1
1	0	0	1	1	1	7	EVEN	2
1	0	1	X	0	1	7	NONE	1
1	0	1	X	1	1	7	NONE	2
1	1	0	0	0	1	8	ODD	1
1	1	0	0	1	1	8	ODD	2
1	1	0	1	0	1	8	EVEN	1
1	1	0	1	1	1	8	EVEN	2
1	1	1	X	0	1	8	NONE	1
1	1	1	X	1	1	8	NONE	2

TBRE (transmitter buffer empty) goes low.

When the transmitter register is empty, the data automatically transfers from the buffer to the register. An output TRE (transmitter register empty) shows the state of the register, being low when the register is in use. The data from the register is now shifted out onto the line with the start, parity and stop bits provided by the UART. The transmission rate is determined by the transmit clock, which should be 16 times the transmit bit rate (e.g. 1760Hz for 110 baud).

The use of a transmit register and buffer and the TBRL, TBRE, TRE signals allows the computer to transmit a continuous data stream with minimum software.

Receive data arrives on RR1 in serial form. The transmission rate is determined by the receive clock which, again, is 16 times the bit rate. The data format is again determined by the mode selection lines. When the character is received, it is loaded into the receive register. Data Ready goes high, and the parity and format are checked. The data can now be read by enabling the tristate output which places the data onto the computer bus. When the data has been read, the processor causes Data Ready Reset to go low which clears Data Ready. The UART is now ready for another character.

There are three error indications. Parity error, obviously indicates that the parity was incorrect (e.g. no stop bit). Overrun indicates that DDR was not set before the next character was received, i.e. the processor was not keeping up with the character stream. Framing Error indicates that the format was wrong (e.g. no stop bit).

The UART needs a certain amount of external logic to decode the port addresses, generate the interrupts on DBE and DR, and handle the various error signals.

6.6.4   The Z-80 SIO

The Z-80 SIO chip is similar in principle to the UART described in the previous section, but has additional facilities. It is designed for interfacing directly to the Z-80 bus, and all the control signals brought out to pins in Fig.6.19 are loaded or read by the CPU via the data bus. Two independent channels are provided, with extra control signals for modems.

The SIO suffers from the pin constraints of the 40 pin package, and no less than three versions are provided with different control signals brought out. All can be used directly with the Z-80 interrupt daisy chain.

At the time of writing (early 1983) the SIO is a rare device in popular microcomputers, the 6402 UART in section 6.6.3 being used instead. In the interests of brevity, no further details of the SIO are given.

6.7 COUNTER TIMER CHIP (CTC)

6.7.1 Introduction

The CTC is a particularly useful member of the Z-80 family. It is used to free the processor of the chore of counting or timing external events. It can be told, for example, "Interrupt the processor in 250mS", or "Interrupt the processor every second", or "Interrupt the processor when 144 items have passed the photocell connected to the CTC counter input". The CTC is therefore ideal for control applications and schemes where timing is important.

The CTC contains four independent circuits, each of which can be used as a counter or a timer.

6.7.2 Channel Operation

The block diagram of one channel is shown on Fig.6.20. The heart of the channel is an 8 bit down counter. An 8 bit number is loaded by the CPU to the time constant register from where it is transferred to the counter.

The counter is decremented either by the system clock or by an external event or clock. When the counter reaches zero, an interrupt is generated, a signal is given to the outside world (to drive a batch counter for example) and the counter reloaded from the time constant register.

If the counter is being used as a timer from the system clock, a pre-scaler is provided to divide the system clock by 256 or 16, selectable by the CPU. With a prescale factor of 256 and the time constant register set for 256, the CTC chip would provide an interrupt every 65.536mS with a 1MHz clock.

The channel control register is loaded by the CPU, and determines the operating mode (external count/clock or system clock, pre-scaler value, positive or negative edge count, interrupt enable/disable etc.).

The full device block diagram is shown on Fig.6.21. The four channels are identical to Fig.6.20, except that channel 3 does not have a zero count output for pin limitations reasons.

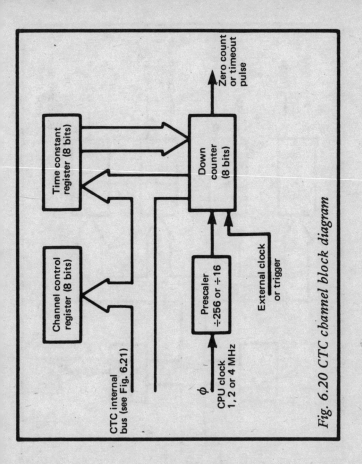

Fig. 6.20 CTC channel block diagram

Each channel is totally independent and has its own interrupt vector.

A channel is configured by writing data to the corresponding channel control register. The channel is selected by two control signals CSO and CSI. These select the channel as follows:

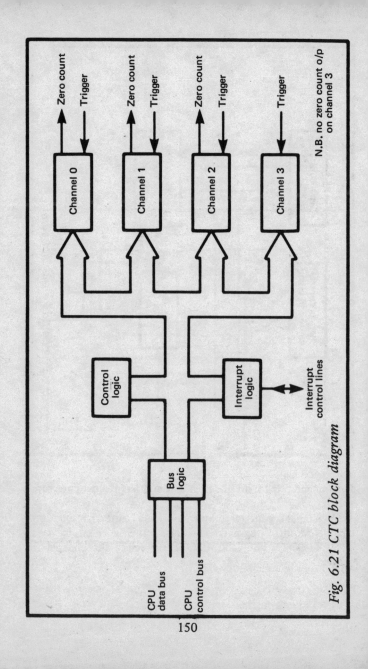

Fig. 6.21 CTC block diagram

	CSI	*CSO*
Channel 0	0	0
Channel 1	0	1
Channel 2	1	0
Channel 3	1	1

Normally the CTC is wired as Fig.6.22, with CSO connected to A0 and CSI connected to Al. Address lines A2 – A7 are decoded to select the CTC chip, so channels 0 – 3 occupy four successive port addresses.

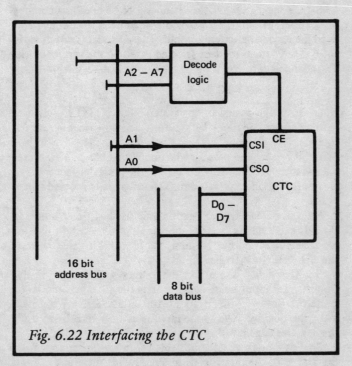

Fig. 6.22 Interfacing the CTC

6.7.3   Programming the CTC

Before the CTC can operate, the channel control register (CCR), time constant register and the interrupt vector have to be loaded for each channel. The channel control register is loaded by writing a word to the channel address (see above) with the format of Fig.6.23.

Bit 0 = '1' shows that this word contains set up data for the CCR. Bit 1 = '1' resets the channel. The channel stops counting or timing until a new time constraint is loaded. The status of the other bits in the CCR is unchanged. This is not the same as a hardware (pin 17) reset. Bit 2 = '1' denotes that the next word written to this channel will be the time constant word.

Bit 6 selects whether the channel is to be used as a counter or a timer. If bit 6 is a '1', the channel is a counter, and decrements on the external input. The prescaler is not used. If Bit 6 is a '0' timer mode is selected based on the system clock. The channels zero count output is a pulse train of period

$$t_c * P * TC$$

where t_c is the period of the system clock, P is the prescaler factor (16 or 256) and TC the time constant (in the range 1 to 256).

Bit 5 selects the prescaler factor. With Bit 5 a '1' the prescaler factor is 256. With Bit 5 a '0' the prescaler factor is 16. Obviously Bit 5 is only relevant if timer mode is selected (Bit 6 = '0').

Bit 3 is called "trigger" and is only used in timer mode. If Bit 3 is a '0', timing starts as soon as the time constant register is loaded. If Bit 3 is a '1' timing starts with a trigger edge on the channels clock/trigger input.

Bit 4 is called slope and determines which edge of the clock/trigger input decrements the counter (in count mode) or starts the timer (in timer mode with Bit 3 at a '1'). With Bit 4 a '1', the positive edge of the input is used. With Bit 4 at a '0', the negative edge is used.

Bit 7 is used to enable or disable the interrupt request. With Bit 7 at a '0' the interrupt is disabled. With Bit 7 at a '1', the interrupt is enabled.

After loading the CCR with Bit 2 = '1', the next word written to a channel must be the time constant. This is an 8 bit number in the range 0 − 256. Numbers 1 − 255 give time

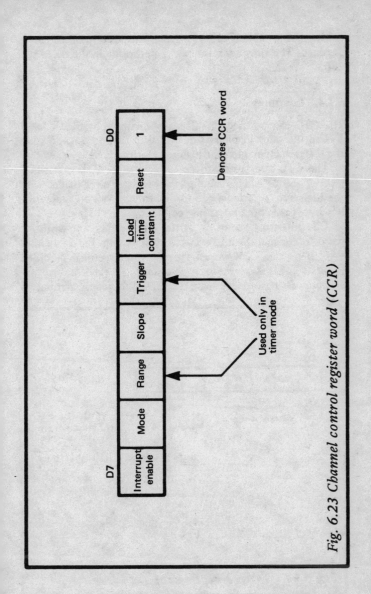

Fig. 6.23 Channel control register word (CCR)

constants 1 — 255. If zero is written, a time constant of 256 is assumed. The time constant can therefore be in the range 1 — 256.

6.7.4 Interrupts

The CTC can be used on the daisy chain with IEI, IEO and INT in the same manner as described in section 6.4.4. Within the CTC, channel 0 has the highest priority.

The CTC is designed to be used with the CPU in mode 2 (see section 6.4). This requires the I register to be loaded with the high byte of a table address, and the device to supply the low byte (called the interrupt vector).

One interrupt vector is written to the CTC by writing a word to channel 0 with Bit 0 = '0' as shown on Fig.6.24 (Bit 1 = '1' denotes a CCR word). This interrupt vector is modified in Bits 1 and 2 as shown for each channel.

Suppose I is loaded with IE, and the vector written to

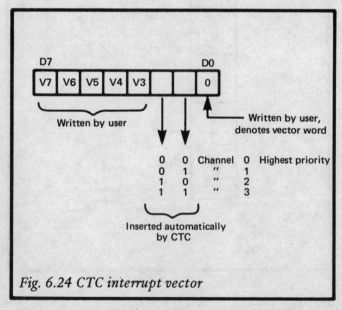

Fig. 6.24 CTC interrupt vector

154

channel 0 is Hex 38 (binary 00111000). The corresponding vectors and table addresses are:

	Vector	Table Address
Channel 1	38	IE38 and IE39
Channel 2	3A	IE3A and IE3B
Channel 3	3C	IE3C and IE3D
Channel 4	3E	IE3E and IE3F

Interrupts are generated when a channel counter reaches zero.

6.7.5 Pin Connections

The CTC pin connections are shown on Fig.6.25. The function of the data bus, M1, RD, IORQ, ϕ, CE, INT, IEI, IEO are identical to the PIO pins in section 6.5.8. CSO and CSI select the channel as outlined above.

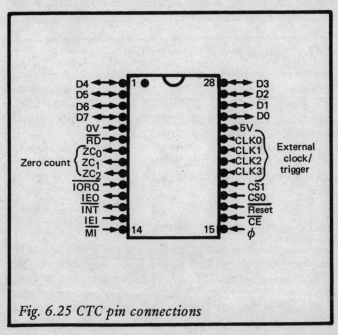

Fig. 6.25 CTC pin connections

Each channel (except 3) has a zero count output (ZC) which strobes high when zero count is reached. Each channel has an input which triggers the counter or initiates the timer.

A low signal to the Reset pin stops all counting and timing, and clears the internal logic. A reset strobe is required on power up to ensure correct operation.

The CTC operates on a single 5 volt rail and draws about 100mA.

6.8 ANALOG INTERFACING

6.8.1 Introduction

Analog signals (i.e. variable voltages) are required for measurement and control applications. There are no specific Z-80 chips, but typical analog input and output circuits are described briefly below.

6.8.2 Digital to Analog Converter (DAC)

As its name implies, the circuit converts a digital output signal from a parallel port to a voltage. Most DACs are based on the R−2R network of Fig.6.26. The output voltage is a representation of the binary state of the switches. In a practical DAC, transistors or FETs are used as switches.

A practical IC is the Ferranti ZN427 DAC. This gives an output in the range 0 to 2.55 volts for a corresponding binary input. The output can, of course, be amplified to any desired level.

6.8.3 Analog to Digital Converter (ADC)

An ADC converts an analog signal to a digital form that can be read by a computer parallel port. A block diagram of a simple ADC is shown on Fig.6.27. A DAC is connected to a counter. The counter is reset by the start pulse which sets FF1, gating pulses to the counter. The DAC output will then be a ramp, which is compared with the input voltage. When the two

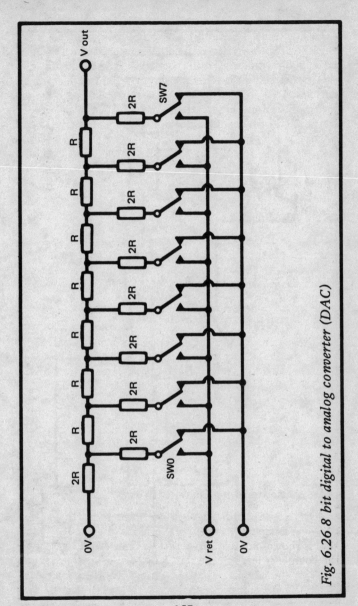

Fig. 6.26 8 bit digital to analog converter (DAC)

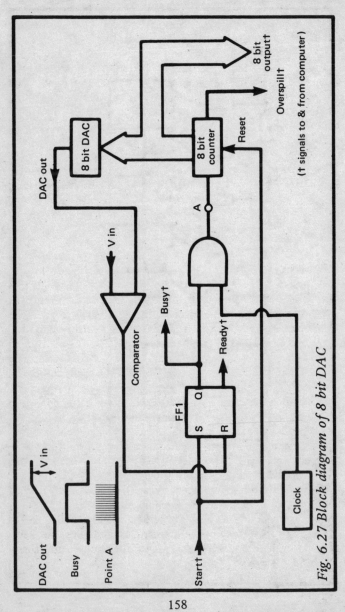

Fig. 6.27 Block diagram of 8 bit DAC

(† signals to & from computer)

8 bit output†

Overspill†

8 bit counter

Reset

8 bit DAC

DAC out

V in

Comparator

A

Busy†

Ready†

FF1

Q

S   R

Start†

Clock

DAC out

Busy

Point A

V in

voltages are equal, the comparator resets FF1, thereby freezing the counter. The counter state is now a digital representation of the input voltage. Ready and Overspill signals are provided which indicate the ADC state to the computer. Usually the port will generate an interrupt on the Ready signal. The Ferranti ZN427 DAC is particularly useful as it contains an 8 bit counter and DAC.

6.8.4   General Observations

The topic of analog interfacing is a very wide one, and cannot be fully covered in a book of this size which is (after all) concerned with the Z-80. Practical DAC and ADC circuits are given in the author's book "Practical Computer Experiments", BP78.

6.9   KEYBOARDS

Every popular microcomputer has a keyboard. These are generally arranged on the matrix principle similar to Fig.6.28. The computer has two I/O ports, an output port driving strobe lines and an input port reading the sense lines.

To read the keyboard, the computer outputs to each strobe line in turn reading back the sense lines for each strobe. On Fig.6.28, for example, if the D key was pressed, we would get the signal on sense line 2 when strobe line 6 was strobed.

Obviously considerable programming effort is needed to scan, read and decode the keyboard. Usually the computer monitor program will have a keyboard read subroutine which can be called by the user. In section 5.8 we used the NASBUG KBD routine as part of our test program.

Keyboards can be scanned by an I/O port address (e.g. Nascom), or by appearing as memory locations (e.g. TRS 80, where store addresses Hex 3801, 3802, 3804, 3808, 3810, 3820, 3840, 3880 provide the strobes and give the keys pressed. There are no actual RAM locations with these addresses).

An alternative approach is to use discrete logic to strobe the

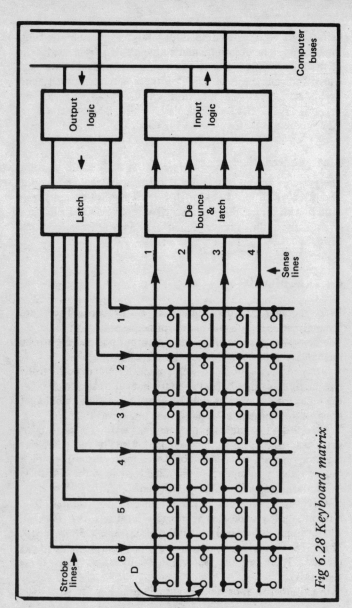

Fig 6.28 Keyboard matrix

keys and scan the sense lines. If a key is pressed, the logic handles the key decoding, and simply presents a 8 bit ASCII code for the computer to read via a parallel port. This method simplifies the programming, but uses quite complex (and hence expensive) logic.

6.10   VDUs

Most microcomputers incorporate a VDU, either built in, using an external monitor or driving a domestic TV. To describe the operation of a VDU in detail would require many pages, involving, as it does, detailed knowledge of how a TV picture is built up. The description below is therefore somewhat simplified, but adequate for a user who wishes to drive a VDU rather than construct one.

A typical VDU will display 16 rows of characters with 48 characters per row. These characters must be stored in the VDU, so the first requirement is some form of store to hold these 744 characters. This will be scanned by some logic to produce the TV picture as Fig.6.29.

To be any use, these store locations must have data written into them. If the VDU is a true peripheral, data will be sent down a serial link (see sections 6.2 and 6.6) and loaded into the store. Control words such as New Line, Carriage Return, Backspace, Cursor Down etc. are sent to determine where characters are placed on the screen.

Most microcomputers, however, use a technique called a Memory Mapped VDU. The character store, shown on Fig.6.30, is a part of the computer store *AND* can be accessed by the VDU logic. The address and data bus can be switched to the computer or VDU display logic, with the computer having priority.

This approach has many advantages. Because the character store is accessed directly by the computer, the VDU is very fast. Each character position on the screen corresponds to one store location, so dynamic display are easily drawn. Less obviously, data can be read back from the screen for use by the program.

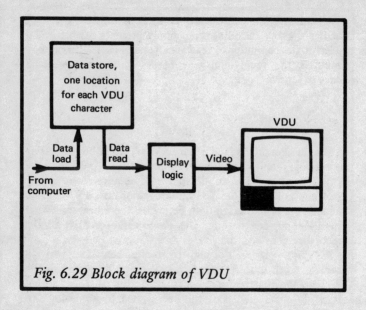

Fig. 6.29 Block diagram of VDU

The Nascom uses a memory mapped VDU, with store locations from Hex 080A (top left) to 0BF9 (bottom right). To display a letter E at the centre of the screen we would write in assembler:

> LD A, £ 45 ; 45 is ASCII E
> LD (£0980), A ; Write to centre of screen

Where a message is to be written, it is usually easier to use the computer monitors VDU subroutine. In the example in section 5.7 the Nascom VDU routine was used.

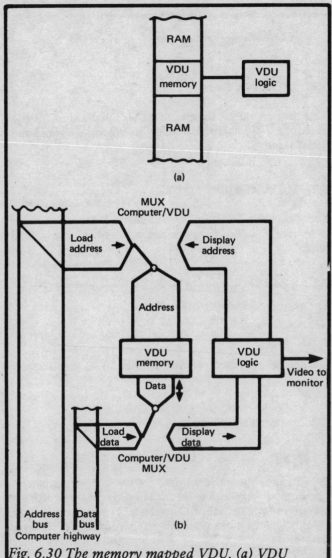

Fig. 6.30 The memory mapped VDU, (a) VDU
memory as part of store, (b) detailed drawing of logic

Chapter Seven

A MISCELLANY OF DATA

7.1 INTRODUCTION

This chapter collects together a rag tag bundle of information about the Z-80, its manufacturers, its support chips and other useful facts.

7.2 SUPPORT CHIPS

The Z-80 has a family of support chips. The commoner ones have been described in earlier chapters. The full (early 1983) family is:

7.2.1 Z-80 CPU

The microprocessor chip itself.

7.2.2 PIO

The parallel input output device described in section 6.5.

7.2.3 CTC

The counter timer chip described in section 6.7.

7.2.4 SIO

A serial input/output controller for use in asynchronous and synchronous applications. Two channels are provided with special control for use with modems. Unlike the commoner UARTs, the SIO can work directly with the Z-80 interrupt daisy chain.

7.2.5 SIO/9

A single channel version of the SIO.

7.2.6 DART

A dual UART for asynchronous serial links.

7.2.7 DMA Controller

DMA stands for direct memory access, and is used where an external device (such as a disc controller or another processor) requires direct access to a computers memory without the intervention of the main processor. A DMA controller handles this transfer. This is not a technique to try without some programming and hardware experience.

7.2.8 FIFO Buffer

The FIFO (for first in/first out) can be considered as a parallel shift register. It is used to provide a 128 word buffer for incoming and outgoing data in I/O and multiprocessor systems. It's use allows the processor to quickly read a "burst" of data that arrived at random intervals of time.

7.2.9 CIO/U

This chip combines the functions of a PIO and CTC chip. It provides two 8 bit parallel ports and a four bit port, plus three counter timer circuits.

7.2.10 Future Developments

As the Z-80 is a development of the 8080, so the Z8000 16 bit micro is a development of the Z-80. Many devices planned for the Z8000 can be used with the Z-80.

7.2.11   Speed

Most Z-80 chips are available in 2MHz or 4MHz versions. The latter are denoted by the suffix A. A lower power version (suffix L) is also available.

7.3   MANUFACTURERS

The original manufacturer is Zilog. The following companies are second source manufacturers:

MOSTEK	(typical device code MK3880)
NEC	(typical device code PD780C)
SGS-ATES	(typical device code Z-80 CPU)
Fairchild	(typical device code F3880)

7.4   TECHNICAL PUBLICATIONS

This book has described the Z-80 in a descriptive, rather than a formal manner. The Zilog publications below give the Z-80 technical and software data in a complete and formal manner, and include details such as bus timing which were considered outside the remit of an introductory book:

a.   Z-80 Technical Manual
b.   Z-80 Programming Manual
c.   PIO Technical Manual
d.   CTC Technical Manual
e.   Zilog Microcomputer Components Data Book

These are all published by Zilog and the second source suppliers.

7.5   Z-80 BASED MICROCOMPUTERS

The following machines use a Z-80 microprocessor:

Altos
Compelec
Cromenco
Exidy Sorceror
Nascom 1 and 2
North Star Horizon
NEC PC-8000
OKI-800
Research Machines 380-Z
Sharp MZ-80
Shelton Signet
Sinclair ZX-80/ZX81/Spectrum
Superbrain
Transam Tuscam
TRS-80
Video Genie

No claim is made for completeness, as new machines are appearing all the time.

7.6 WRITING A PROGRAM

The beginner should not start by writing a 16K machine code program; that way lies madness and divorce! It is better to first start by writing simple programs to, say, add two numbers and display the result on the screen. When confidence is gained, progress to more ambitious programs can be made.

The stages in writing a program are usually as follows:

a.   Define what needs to be done, and if possible break the program down into digestible blocks (e.g. Keyboard Input, Update Members Addresses, Identify Overdue Accounts). This stops the task overwhelming the programmer!

b.   Draw up flowcharts as we did in section 5.5. These should start off relatively simple, then be made more detailed until they can be translated to program instructions. Try to identify useful subroutines (e.g. multiplication, division, sorts, searches, etc.) and build up a sub-routine library. Do not re-invent the wheel with every program!

c. With detailed flow charts, draw up a source program in Assembler Code *EVEN* if you are using a monitor to load the machine code program. It is worth it for the clear documentation it provides when the inevitable de-bugging occurs.

d. Translate the source program to an object program, either with an assembler or by hand.

e. *MAKE A COPY OF THE OBJECT PROGRAM* on tape or disc before attempting to run it. Very few machine code programs run first time, and a single error can cause a program to self destruct.

f. Cross your fingers and run your program. Do not be disheartened if it does not run first time. Use the monitor program's breakpoint and single step routines to check the program operation.

7.7 BASIC and PEEK and POKE

It is possible to intermingle BASIC and machine code programs, and the technique is particularly useful where a program requires complex calculations (which are done in BASIC) and fast I/O or VDU graphics (which are done in machine code).

Most BASICs allow the program to call a machine code subroutine. The commonest BASIC instructions are CALL and USR. There are differences between dialects of BASIC, but, for example, the BASIC instruction:

CALL 1519

will call the machine code program at decimal address 1519. The machine code program is required to be terminated with a RET instruction which resumes BASIC at the instruction after the CALL.

It is possible, but laborious, to load a machine code

program via BASIC using the POKE instruction. An object program is converted, by hand, a location at a time from Hex to decimal, then included as DATA statements in the BASIC program. These are READ and POKE'd by a FOR-NEXT loop.

Data in store locations that have been used by the machine code program can be examined by the BASIC program via the PEEK function.

Setting up a machine code program via BASIC is obviously tedious, but is useful for small subroutines and obviates the need to load a BASIC and machine code program separately.

When deciding where a machine code program is to reside along with BASIC, due care should be taken to avoid a clash. Most computers have a "Memory Map" which shows what store addresses are used for what. Usually the store used by BASIC can be restricted with a SIZE or similar statement.

7.8   THE INTEL 8080

As explained earlier, the Z-80 is a development of the 8080, and as a result 8080 programs will run on a Z-80. The reverse is not, however, necessarily true. The tables in Chapter 4 identify the 8080 compatible instructions.

The programmers model of the 8080 is shown on Fig.7.1. As can be seen it is almost a half Z-80, having no alternate register set, no I or R registers, and no index registers. Needless to say, the 8080 has fewer instructions.

Although 8080 programs will run on the Z-80, there are usually a few practical problems. The first concerns the running of even Z-80 programs on different machines. All computers use different ways of driving keyboards, VDUs etc., so there are problems moving a Z-80 machine code program, from, say, a TRS-80 to a Nascom. This problem is compounded with the 8080, as the whole configuration of the original computer may be different.

The second problem concerns 8080 source programs. Unfortunately 8080 Assembler Mnemonics bear little, if any, resemblance to Z-80 Mnemonics. For example:

Fig. 7.1 Programmers model of the Intel 8080

8080	Z-80
MOV	LD
INR	INC
XCHG	EX

Although the resulting object program will be the same, translating an 8080 source program to a Z-80 source program can be an infuriating experience. Out of fairness, it should be said that the Zilog designers did not instigate change for changes sake. The Z-80 mnemonics are far more logical and easier to remember than the 8080 mnemonics.

Intel have produced their own enhanced version of the 8080, called the 8085. There is very little compatibility between the 8085 and the Z-80.

Appendix A

BINARY AND HEXADECIMAL NUMBERS

We are so used to working in decimal numbers that we tend to take it for granted, and consider our way of counting to be the only way possible. Basically we count in "tens", and our number system is said to operate to a "base" of ten. The number, 4059, for example means:

	4 thousands	i.e. 4 x 10 x 10 x 10
+	0 hundreds,	i.e. 0 x 10 x 10
+	5 tens,	i.e. 5 x 10
+	9 units,	i.e. 9 x 1

There is no reason why we should count to a base of ten except, of course, that we have ten fingers. A counting system can be devised to any base. Ten is, actually, a rather bad choice as ten can only be divided by five and two. Trade would have been simpler if we had twelve fingers, as twelve can be divided by four, three, two and six, and is a "packable" number in that twelve items can be neatly packed four by three or two by two by three.

Two number systems are of particular interest in computing; Base two, known as Binary, and Base sixteen, known as Hexadecimal, or Hex for short. We will deal with Hex first as it is conceptually the simplest.

To count in Hex we need sixteen symbols (including zero). These are the numerals $0 - 9$ and the letters $A - F$.

Decimal	0 1 2 3 4 5 6 7 8 9 10 11 12 13 14 15
Hex	0 1 2 3 4 5 6 7 8 9 A B C D E F

What happens now? We simply start a new Hex column:

Decimal	16 17 18 19 20 21 . . . . . . 29 30 31 32 33 etc.
Hex	10 11 12 13 14 15 . . . . . . 1D 1E 1F 20 21 etc.

We can also, of course, construct large numbers.

171

1DF6, for example, means

	1 x sixteen x sixteen x sixteen	=	4096
+	D (thirteen) x sixteen x sixteen	=	3328
+	F (fifteen) x sixteen	=	240
+	6	=	6

7670 in decimal

There are many ways of converting from decimal to Hex, but one of the simplest is to note the powers of 16 up to 65536:

16, 256, 4096

Conversions of numbers above 65536 are rarely required in computing. The method is best described by example:

e.g. 53156
First divide by 4096 gives 12 (C) remainder 4004
Now divide 4004 by 256, which gives 15 (F) remainder 164
Now divide 164 by 16, which gives 10 (A) remainder 4

The Hex equivalent of 53156 is therefore CFA4.

Hex is, itself, little more than a mathematical curiosity, but as we shall see later, it can be used as a convenient way to represent binary numbers.

Binary is a number system to a base of two. It has only two symbols: 0 and 1. As each column in a decimal number represents a power of ten, so each column in a binary number represents a power of two (1, 2, 4, 8, 16 etc.)

We thus count:

Decimal	Binary
	8 4 2 1
0	0 0 0 0
1	0 0 0 1
2	0 0 1 0
3	0 0 1 1
4	0 1 0 0
5	0 1 0 1

172

6	0 1 1 0
7	0 1 1 1
8	1 0 0 0

and so on.

A typical binary number is therefore 1 0 1 1 0 1 1 0 (conventionally, the least significant end is to the right, the same as decimal numbers). To convert this to decimal we simply write the corresponding powers of two:

1	1 x 2 x 2 x 2 x 2 x 2 x 2 x 2	128
0	0 x 2 x 2 x 2 x 2 x 2 x 2	0
1	1 x 2 x 2 x 2 x 2 x 2	32
1	1 x 2 x 2 x 2 x 2	16
0	0 x 2 x 2 x 2	0
1	1 x 2 x 2	4
1	1 x 2	2
0	0 x 1	0
		182

The decimal equivalent of 1 0 1 1 0 1 1 10 is therefore 182

The simplest way to convert from decimal to binary is to use repeated division by two, noting the remainder each time. For example, to convert decimal 57 to binary:

Dividing by two each time we get:

57	28	remainder 1
28	14	remainder 0
14	7	remainder 0
7	3	remainder 1
3	1	remainder 1
1	0	remainder 1

The remainders are read with least significant at the top to give the binary number 1 1 1 0 0 1 which is equivalent to decimal 57.

The 1s and 0s of binary are particularly easy to represent with electronic circuits, so all computers work internally in binary. Unfortunately, large binary numbers such as:

1011001101111001

are difficult to comprehend, and even more difficult to remember. This is where Hex is useful.

Conversion between binary and Hex is very easy. The binary number is split into groups of four bits. Each group of four bits can represent a number from 0 to fifteen, or Hex 0 to F. The Hex representation of each group is then written down to give the corresponding Hex number. Taking our example above

	1011001101111001			
Split into groups of four	1011	0011	0111	1001
Hex equivalents	B	3	7	9

The Hex number is therefore B379

The reverse conversion is equally easy. The Hex number is written down and the four binary bits corresponding to each digit put below, e.g. 85F6

8	5	F	6
1000	0101	1111	0110

The binary number is therefore 1 0 0 0 0 1 0 1 1 1 1 1 0 1 1 0

Most microprocessor instructions are usually given in Hex. This is purely for the convenience of the programmer, the computer itself works in binary.

The microprocessor user usually need not concern himself with the mechanics of binary arithmetic. Full details (and circuit) are given in "Practical Computer Experiments" BP 78. A few practical points, however, are worth noting.

The rules of binary addition are very simple:

$$0 \, . \, + \, 1 = 1$$
$$1 \, + \, 0 = 1$$
$$0 \, + \, 0 = 0$$
$$1 \, + \, 1 = 0 \text{ plus carry to next bit}$$

For example

```
  10110011
+ 00100101
  --------
  11011000
```

The carry flag in the flag register is set if an arithmetic

operation overspills 8 bits. For example:

$$
\begin{array}{r}
1\,0\,1\,1\,0\,0\,1\,1 \\
+\,1\,0\,1\,0\,0\,1\,0\,1 \\
\hline
\end{array}
$$

Carry1 0 1 0 1 1 0 0 0

This allows 16 bit arithmetic to be performed.

An 8 bit number can be used to represent a decimal number in the range 0 to 255, or, by designating the top bit to indicate sign, a number in the range −128 to + 127.

Before we see how this is done, let us consider a decimal analogy. Consider the sum:

$$
\begin{array}{r}
0\,2\,3 \\
+\,9\,9\,4 \\
\hline
1\,0\,1\,7
\end{array}
$$

If we ignore the thousand column, the answer is 17. The number 994 thus looks like minus 6. Another example:

$$
\begin{array}{r}
2\,5\,1 \\
+\,8\,2\,7 \\
\hline
1\,0\,7\,8
\end{array}
$$

Again, ignoring the thousand column, the answer is 78. The number 827 looks like minus 173.

A three digit decimal negative number is formed by subtraction from one thousand. Minus 6 is then 1000 − 6 = 994.

Negative binary numbers can be formed in a similar manner. Consider the sum:

$$
\begin{array}{rl}
0\,1\,1\,0 & 6 \\
1\,1\,0\,0 & \\
\hline
1\,0\,0\,1\,0 & 2
\end{array}
$$

The number 1100 thus represents minus 4

It is very easy to produce a negative number in binary. Take the number, complement it (i.e. replace '1's by '0's and vice versa) then add 1.

e.g.

0 0 0 0 0 1 1 0	6 (to 8 bits)
1 1 1 1 1 0 0 1	Complemented
1 1 1 1 1 0 1 0	Add 1

1 1 1 1 1 0 1 0 thus represents minus 6 in 8 bits.

In general, the top bit is a '1' if the number is negative, and '0' if it is positive.

The above representation is known as twos complement arithmetic.

It should be emphasied that the programmer can use an 8 bit number as an 8 bit unsigned number or an 8 bit twos complement number to suit his needs.

Appendix B

Z-80 INSTRUCTION SET

This appendix gives the complete Z-80 instructions set in Assembler Mnemonic Form. Reference should also be made to the tables in Chapter 4.

The following notation is used:

N	Single Byte Data
NN	Double Byte Data
( )	Store Address or I/O Address
R	Register
A	Accumulator
D	Offset (not available on some instructions)
SS	Register Pair
CC	Conditions

Conditions

C	Carry
NC	No Carry
Z	Zero
NZ	Non Zero
PE	Parity Even
PO	Parity Odd
M	Sign Neg
P	Sign Pos
ADC	HL,SS	Add with Carry Reg. Pair SS to HL
ADC	A,S	Add with Carry Operand S to Acc
ADD	A,N	Add Value N to Acc
ADD	A,R	Add Reg. R to Acc
ADD	A,(HL)	Add Location (HL) to Acc
ADD	A,(IX+D)	Add Location (IX+D) to Acc
ADD	A,(IY+D)	Add Location (IY+D) to Acc
ADD	IX,SS	Add Reg. Pair SS to IX
ADD	IY,SS	Add Reg. Pair SS to IY
ADD	IY,RR	Add Reg. Pair RR to IY
AND	S	Logical 'AND' of Operand S and Acc
BIT	B,(HL)	Test Bit B of Location (HL)
BIT	B,(IX+D)	Test Bit B of Location (IX+D)
BIT	B,(IY+D)	Test Bit B of Location (IY+D)

BIT	B,R	Test Bit B of Reg. R
CALL	CC,NN	Call subroutine at Location NN if Condition CC is true
CALL	NN	Unconditional Call subroutine at Location NN
CCF		Complement Carry Flag
CP	S	Compare Operand S with Acc
CPD		Compare Location (HL) and Acc Decrement HL and BC until CB=0
CPDR		Compare Location (HL) and Acc Decrement HL and BC, repeat
CPI		Compare Location (HL) and Acc. Increment HL and Decrement BC
CPIR		Compare Location (HL) and Acc. Increment HL, Decrement BC Repeat until BC=0
CPL		Complement Acc. (1's comp)
DAA		Decimal Adjust Acc
DEC	M	Decrement Operand M
DEC	IX	Decrement IX
DEC	IY	Decrement IY
DEC	SS	Decrement Reg. Pair SS
DI		Disable Interrupts
DJNZ	B	Decrement B and Jump Relative if B=0
EI		Enable Interrupts
EX	(SP),HL	Exchange the Location (SP) and HL
EX	(SP),IX	Exchange the Location (SP) and IX
EX	(SP),IY	Exchange the Location (SP) and IY
EX	AF,AF′	Exchange the contents of AF and AF′
EX	DE,HL	Exchange the contents of DE and HL
EXX		Exchange the contents of BC, DE, HL with contents of BC′, DE′, HL′ respectively
HALT		Halt (wait for Interrupt or Reset)
IM	0	Set Interrupt Mode 0
IM	1	Set Interrupt Mode 1
IM	2	Set Interrupt Mode 2
IN	A,(N)	Load the Acc. with input from device N
IN	R,(C)	Load the Reg. R with input from device (C)
INC	(HL)	Increment Location (HL)
INC	IX	Increment IX

INC	(IX+D)	Increment Location (IX+D)
INC	IY	Increment IY
INC	(IY+D)	Increment Location (IY+D)
INC	R	Increment Reg. R.
INC	SS	Increment Reg. Pair SS
IND		Load Location (HL) with input from Port (C), Decrement HL and B
INDR		Load Location (HL) with input from Port (C), Decrement HL and Decrement B, repeat until B=0
INI		Load Location (HL) with input from Port (C), and Increment HL and Decrement B
INIR		Load Location (HL) with input from Port (C), and Increment HL and Decrement B, repeat until B=0
JP	(HL)	Unconditional Jump to (HL)
JP	(IX)	Unconditional Jump to (IX)
JP	(IY)	Unconditional Jump to (IY)
JP	CC,NN	Jump to Location NN if condition CC is true
JP	NN	Unconditional Jump to Location NN
JP	C,E	Jump relative to PC+E if Carry =1
JR	E	Unconditional Jump relative to PC+E
JR	NC,E	Jump relative to PC+E if Carry =0
JR	NZ,E	Jump relative to PC+E if Non Zero (Z=0)
JR	Z,E	Jump relative to PC+E if Zero (Z=1)
LD	A,(BC)	Load Acc, with Location (BC)
LD	A,(DE)	Load Acc. with Location (DE)
LD	A,I	Load Acc. with I
LD	A,(NN)	Load Acc. with Location NN
LD	A,R	Load Acc. with Reg. R
LD	(BC),A	Load Location (BC) with Acc.
LD	(DE),A	Load Location (DE) with Acc.
LD	(HL),N	Load Location (HL) with value N
LD	DD,NN	Load Reg. Pair DD with value NN
LD	HL,(NN)	Load HL with Location (NN)
LD	(HL),R	Load location (HL) with Reg. R
LD	I,A	Load I with Acc.
LD	IX,NN	Load IX with value NN
LD	IX,(NN)	Load IX with Location (NN)

LD	(IX+D),N	Load Location (IX+D) with value N
LD	(IX+D),R	Load Location (IX+D) with Reg. R
LD	IY,NN	Load IY with value NN
LD	IY,(NN)	Load IY with Location (NN)
LD	(IY+D),N	Load Location (IY+D) with value N
LD	(IY+D),R	Load Location (IY+D) with Reg. R
LD	(NN),A	Load Location (NN) with Acc.
LD	(NN),DD	Load Location (NN) with Reg. Pair DD
LD	(NN),HL	Load Location (NN) with HL
LD	(NN),IX	Load Location (NN) with IX
LD	(NN),IY	Load Location (NN) with IY
LD	R,A	Load R with Acc.
LD	R,(HL)	Load Reg. R with Location (HL)
LD	R,(IX+D)	Load Reg. R with Location (IX+D)
LD	R,(IY+D)	Load Reg. R with Location (IY+D)
LD	R,N	Load Reg. R with value N
LD	R,R′	Load Reg. R with Reg. R′
LD	SP,HL	Load SP with HL
LD	SP,IX	Load SP with IX
LD	SP,IY	Load SP with IY
LDD		Load Location (DE) with Location (HL), Decrement DE, HL and BC
LDDR		Load Location (DE) with Location (HL), Decrement DE, HL and BC, repeat until BC=0
LDI		Load Location (DE) with Location (HL), Increment DE, HL, Decrement BC
LDIR		Load Location (DE) with Location (HL), Increment DE, HL, Decrement BC and repeat until BC=0
NEG		Negate Acc. (2's complement)
NOP		No Operation
OR	S	Logical 'OR' of operand S and Acc.
OTDR		Load Output Port (C) with Location (HL), Decrement HL and B, repeat until B=0
OTIR		Load Output Port (C) with Location (HL), Increment HL, Decrement B, repeat until B=0
OUT	(C),R	Load Output Port (C) with Reg. R

OUT	(N),A	Load Output Port (N) with Acc.
OUTD		Load Output Port (C) with Location (HL), Decrement HL and B
OUTI		Load Output Port (C) with Location (HL), Increment HL and Decrement B
POP	IX	Load IX with top of stack
POP	IY	Load IY with top of stack
POP	SS	Load Reg. Pair SS with top of stack
PUSH	IX	Load IX onto stack
PUSH	IY	Load IY onto stack
PUSH	SS	Load Reg. Pair SS onto stack
RES	B,M	Reset Bit B of Operand M
RET		Return from subroutine
RET	CC	Return from subroutine if condition CC is true
RETI		Return from Interrupt
RETN		Return from Non Maskable Interrupt
RL	M	Rotate Left through Carry Operand M
RL		Rotate Left Acc. through Carry
RLC	(HL)	Rotate Location (HL) left circular
RLC	(IX+D)	Rotate Location (IX+D) left circular
RLC	(IY+D)	Rotate Location (IY+D) left circular
RLC	R	Rotate Reg. R left circular
RLCA		Rotate left circular Acc.
RLD		Rotate Digit left and right between Acc. and Location (HL)
RR	M	Rotate right through Carry Operand M
RRA		Rotate right Acc. through Carry
RRC	M	Rotate Operand M right circular
RRCA		Rotate right circular Acc.
RRD		Rotate digit right and left between Acc. and Location (HL)
RST	P	Restart to Location P
SBC	A,S	Subtract operand S from Acc. with Carry
SBC	HL,SS	Subtract Reg. pair SS from HL with Carry
SCF		Set Carry Flag (C=1)
SET	B,(HL)	Set Bit B of Location (HL)
SET	B,(IX+D)	Set Bit B of Location (IX+D)
SET	B,(IY+D)	Set Bit B of Location (IY+D)

SET	B,R	Set Bit B of Reg. R
SLA	M	Shift operand M left arithmetic
SRA	M	Shift operand M right arithmetic
SRL	M	Shift operand M right logical
SUB	S	Subtract operand S from Acc.
XOR	S	Exclusive 'OR' operand S and Acc.

Pseudo Instructions

ORG	NN	Sets Location counter (LC) to NN
EQU	NN	Assigns value NN to Label
DEFS	E	Increments LC by value of expression E
DEFB	E(,E)...	Defines Byte (s) as E
DEFW	E(,E)...	Defines Word (s) as E
DEFM	/S/	Assigns String S to label

Appendix C

ASCII CHARACTER CODES

DEC	HEX	CHAR		DEC	HEX	CHAR
32	20			64	40	@
33	21	!		65	41	A
34	22	"		66	42	B
35	23	#		67	43	C
36	24	$		68	44	D
37	25	%		69	45	E
38	26	&		70	46	F
39	27	ʼ		71	47	G
40	28	(		72	48	H
41	29	)		73	49	I
42	2A	*		74	4A	J
43	2B	+		75	4B	K
44	2C	,		76	4C	L
45	2D	-		77	4D	M
46	2E	.		78	4E	N
47	2F	/		79	4F	O
48	30	0		80	50	P
49	31	1		81	51	Q
50	32	2		82	52	R
51	33	3		83	53	S
52	34	4		84	54	T
53	35	5		85	55	U
54	36	6		86	56	V
55	37	7		87	57	W
56	38	8		88	58	X
57	39	9		89	59	Y
58	3A	:		90	5A	Z
59	3B	;		91	5B	[
60	3C	<		92	5C	\
61	3D	=		93	5D	]
62	3E	>		94	5E	^
63	3F	?		95	5F	_

DEC	HEX	CHAR		DEC	HEX	CHAR
96	60	`		112	70	p
97	61	a		113	71	q
98	62	b		114	72	r
99	63	c		115	73	s
100	64	d		116	74	t
101	65	e		117	75	u
102	66	f		118	76	v
103	67	g		119	77	w
104	68	h		120	78	x
105	69	i		121	79	y
106	6A	j		122	7A	z
107	6B	k		123	7B	{
108	6C	l		124	7C		
109	6D	m		125	7D	}
110	6E	n		126	7E	~
111	6F	o		127	7F	▓

Codes less than Decimal 32 are control codes
Common are (in Decimal):

```
07 Bell
10 Line Feed
12 Form Feed
13 Carraige Return
```